Mounted Infantry
At War

1   In the face of a storm

Mounted Infantry At War

Capt Stratford St Leger

GALAGO

© (This edition) Galago Publishing (Pty) Ltd
Book and cover design Francis Lategan
All Rights Reserved
ISBN 0 947020 22 5

First published as WAR SKETCHES IN COLOUR by A & C Black in
1903.
This edition the text reproduced as a facsimile of the first edition and
published by Galago in May 1986
Galago books are published by Galago Publishing (Pty) Ltd
P O Box 404, Alberton 1450 RSA

Colour and black and white reproduction by Citygraphics,
Johannesburg

Printed and bound by CTP Book Printers

FOREWORD

On the 11th October 1899, the Transvaal and Orange Free State went to war with Great Britain.

Britain anticipated a quick victory, certainly not expecting volunteer Boer farmers, self equipped and in the European sense untrained for war, to be able to hold out for long against the might of the British Army, an army that had not suffered a serious reverse since they had beaten Napoleon at Waterloo in 1815, eighty five years before.

They couldn't have been more wrong, for two weeks later after five distinct actions had been fought, the score was one vague win, two actions that had been indecisive, one a definite loss and the last a total disaster.

In addition twelve thousand British troops were locked up in Ladysmith by besieging boer commandos. Mafeking and Kimberley were likewise besieged, and it looked as if they would fall any time the Boers decided to mount a serious attack.

On the 12th November 1899, General Lord Methuen assembled a fighting column of eight thousand troops at the Orange River for the purpose of relieving Kimberley.

Gone was a lot of the ridiculous optimism that had characterised the early British efforts, replacing it was the beginnings of a new professionalism that has been the hallmark of the British Army throughout history, once it has suffered a major defeat.

The author, a captain and a company commander of a

FOREWORD

mounted infantry unit, for many foot soldiers had by then already been mounted so they could fight the highly mobile boer commandos on equal terms, started his war at De Aar.

His unit, like the rest of the relieving troops, travelled light and neither tents nor comforts were permitted to officers or men, each carrying on his horse only one hundred and twenty rounds of ammunition, a shirt, a pair of socks, a pair of drawers, a holdall, boot laces, a rubber curry comb and brush, a sponge, a towel, soap, an emergency ration, a canteen and one day's supply of oats for the horse. The supply wagons carried, one blanket, one ground sheet, one greatcoat and one jersey per man.

It took the column until the 15th February 1900 to reach Kimberley and relieve the town. In between this time the British Army suffered two further major catastrophes with the defeats of General Gatacre at Stormberg and General Buller at Colenso.

From Kimberley the author took part in the occupation of Bloemfontein and finally the occupation of Pretoria.

Captain St Leger was a keen observer and his written anecdotes of the various actions in which he took part make fascinating reading.

More importantly, however, was his artistic talent which he put to good use in the production of many paintings during the march and the prints of which, in both colour and black and white, illustrate this most beautiful classic of the Boer War.

Little is known of the author, but according to a pencilled note within the volume from which this edition was facsimiled, he, like so many others of his generation, was tragically killed in action during the Battle of the Somme in 1916.

Peter Stiff

PREFACE

THESE sketches have in no sense the slightest pretensions to being a history of any phase of the Boer War. They are merely an attempt to depict a few of the more interesting and some of the lesser known episodes in the advance to Pretoria, as seen by a company officer who had the good fortune to serve with the Mounted Infantry attached to General French's 1st Cavalry Brigade.

Histories innumerable of the war have appeared, written both by those qualified to do so and also by others who certainly were not. Had I attempted more than these slight sketches I should have come under the latter heading. Any attempt to write a history of a war or to criticise the actions of its generals, without the writer being fully in possession of the facts and having complete access to all the information on which their orders were based, can serve no good end, and would be worthless for the purpose intended, and possibly harmful.

This volume is the outcome of a sketch book, kept up from day to day during the war, with the idea of, perhaps, enabling me to add a few pictures, that might possibly prove of interest, to the Mounted Infantry scrap-book; at the time, however, the idea of publishing these sketches in book form never for a moment entered my head.

I have endeavoured to leave out unnecessary detail that would only prove irksome to all except the students of military history, to whom this book will be of no interest.

It is difficult, and I have found it impossible, in a book of reminiscences such as this, to ignore myself as completely as I should have wished.

I am indebted to an old school-fellow for the account of the Siege of Kimberley; and to one who, as a Burgher of the Transvaal, fought on the Boer side, for the data on which the sketch of Life on Commando is founded.

I have been enabled, through the courtesy of the proprietors of *Black and White*, to make use of many of my original sketches which formed the foundation for pictures in that paper.

S. E. ST LEGER.

2nd November 1903.

CONTENTS

FULL PAGE ILLUSTRATIONS

Black and White

FULL PAGE ILLUSTRATIONS

FULL PAGE ILLUSTRATIONS

THE RELIEF OF KIMBERLEY

THE RELIEF OF KIMBERLEY

I SHALL endeavour to describe some experiences of the men who actually rode into Kimberley with the relief column under General French.

The ride was one of the most exciting experiences of the war. Every man in the column knew what our objective was, and, stirred by the accounts of the suffering of the women and children in the besieged town, realised that what we were attempting had to be done at all costs, and done quickly.

Before describing the actual ride, I ought perhaps to give some account of our work for the three weeks previous to our concentration at Ramdam on February 11, 1900.

Colonel Alderson's Mounted Infantry had, after their arrival in South Africa on November 11, 1899, been for the most part at De Aar, chafing under the monotonous inactivity of their life, unrelieved by any excitement, with the exception of occasional patrols to Philipstown, an expedition to Prieska, and guarding the Hanover Road railway bridge.   I speak of Colonel Alderson's Mounted Infantry, because that was the name we were generally known by.   As a matter of fact, however, Colonel Alderson never commanded us (the 1st Mounted Infantry Regiment) as a regiment after we left Aldershot.   Once in South Africa, he was given the command of a brigade of mounted infantry made up of regulars and colonials.

The Hanover Road railway bridge has become interesting as being the spot where over two years later Kritzinger was captured—in consequence, I believe, of his pluckily riding back to rescue a wounded man.

Being on detachment at Hanover Road was quite a welcome change from De Aar.   Here, at anyrate, we had a river to bathe in, and there was generally some little excitement in trying to head off occasional Boer scouts who worked their way across from Colesberg, which is about thirty-five miles distant.

Once a week we received a visit from some of the residents at Hanover, who drove over with their wives.   These good people were most generous, and always brought a large consignment of cakes, bread, fruit, matches, and cigarettes for the men.

Hanover Road recalls a story told to me by the storekeeper there, who, with his charming wife, was most hospitable to us. He was paying some Kaffirs who had been employed by him their week's wages. One man, after expostulating for some time at the amount he had received, which

Hanover Road railway bridge.

was not at all in accordance with the somewhat exalted ideas he entertained of his worth as a labourer, held the money out in the outstretched palm of his hand, and, contemptuously gazing at it, said, " Call this Hanover Road ! I call it h—l of a road."

This serves to show how impudent the natives become, if unchecked, and also their ready command of the English language.

One company was also detached from De Aar
for duty at the Orange River bridge, and there,
shortly after our arrival, we sustained our first
loss.   One morning a gloom was cast over our
camp by the sad news that Captain Bradshaw,
of the York and Lancaster Regiment, commanding this company, and two of his men had
been killed at Ramah, just across the Orange
Free State border.   At the same time Lieutenant
Gregson of the Buffs and two or three of his men
were seriously wounded.

Gregson had a very uncomfortable experience,
as he was lying there with a shattered thigh, and
two of his men wounded on either side of him.
Unable to move, the three were repeatedly fired
at.   The man on Gregson's right was hit a
second time by a bullet in the head, and instantly
killed; the other also was hit again, but, happily,
with no serious result.

Poor Bradshaw, whose career was so abruptly
cut short, was a great favourite with everyone, and
had only left us with his company a few days
previously, full of enthusiasm and keenness to
get a little nearer to the front.

Possibly it was over-zealousness that caused his
death; but that this mishap should have been

2   A prisoner

3 Outpost breakfast

instantly, as it was, put down to, and used as a warning against, the lack of proper scouting, appeared to those who know the facts unjust and uncalled for—as were many of the sweeping charges of this description that throughout the war were made against the army as a whole. The Boer commando which Bradshaw had been sent out to locate lost their leader, the field-cornet, at this little skirmish; but I don't think his death provoked the same criticism.

De Aar, which is about seventy miles from the Orange River and sixty miles as the crow flies from Colesberg, is the junction for all trains to Cape Town and Port Elizabeth from Kimberley and the north, and also for those from Bloemfontein and Pretoria to Cape Town.

At the time we arrived there, in November 1899, the garrison was but a small one. When one considers the value to us of the huge quantity of stores and ammunition, and the number of remounts, that had been collected there, it seems inexplicable that the Boers made no attempt to capture such an important junction and supply depot. It is true that we held the Orange River bridge. They, however, were in possession of Norval's Pont bridge and Colesberg, which is

practically only a ride from De Aar. It shows
how thoroughly they were kept occupied by
General French, operating from Naauwpoort, that
no attempt was made, if not actually to attack De
Aar, at any rate to cut the line between it and
the Orange River bridge. If they had grasped the
importance of the position to us, they no doubt
would have made every effort to pour into the
colony over Norval's Pont bridge a force strong
enough to threaten us both at Naauwpoort and at
De Aar. Had they cut our lines of communication north of De Aar, Lord Methuen's force, with
Cronje holding him in front and his supplies cut off
in rear, would have been in no enviable position.

The Boers, happily for us, preferred sitting
round Mafeking, Kimberley, and Ladysmith.

Although living in comparative comfort at De
Aar, having tents and all the useless campaign-
ing kit that we had taken out with us, we were
exceedingly glad to leave these behind, get away
from the place, and feel that we were doing our
share of active work. We did not see tents again,
with the exception of a few days at Bloemfontein,
until October 28, over nine months later.

De Aar is chiefly impressed on our minds by the
heat, dust, and flies. In the pitiless, bare, and

parched veldt a railway station, a church, and a
few small houses have been planted, without shade
or shelter of any kind, with the exception of a few
blue gums which have grown up with the buildings. Several isolated ironstone kopjes covered
with stunted bush are dotted about to the east,
south, and west of this uninviting spot.

The weak points in our line of defence at De
Aar were connected by strong wire-fencing and

De Aar.

small redoubts; one of these will be seen in the
sketch above. Our horses on the left are having a
quiet day's grazing. The shimmering heat rising
off the bare veldt reflects distant objects on its
surface, as though it were a huge sheet of glass.

It was with feelings of great relief that we got
orders to leave on January 22 with a flying column
under Colonel Alderson for Prieska. The marching-
out state of my company was 138 officers and men,
151 horses; these numbers had dwindled down to

55 officers and men and 63 horses fit to move out of Silverton Camp, Pretoria, on June 8 following.

We left De Aar as light as possible : all that the transport carried was one blanket, one waterproof sheet, one greatcoat, and one jersey per man. On the horse were carried—in wallets—120 rounds of ammunition, one shirt, one pair socks, one pair drawers, hold-all, bootlaces, rubber curry-comb and brush, sponge, towel, soap, and emergency ration, also canteen on off wallet. One day's supply of oat-hay and oats was carried on the horse as well.

Later at Bloemfontein we managed to get another blanket per man, which was sorely needed. A cold night in the veldt with only one blanket is not an experience I should like to go through again. At one time I lost my blankets, and for a fortnight I tried sleeping with one which I borrowed ; between two and three o'clock each night I woke up with the intense cold and found it quite impossible to sleep again—the only thing to be done was to get up and walk about, and in this way endeavour to keep warm. One night I thought I had done myself really well, and crept under a huge buck-waggon cover ; this, however, I soon found to be quite a mistake, as the cold, biting wind went through the covering as if it were made of muslin.

Of the kit we left at De Aar many of us never saw the greater portion again; personally I lost everything except the least important part of it, a compactum bed. Our mess stores also fared badly. I remember one case of whisky, if not more, that subsequently reached us at Bloemfontein, arriving with the bottles full of water; the bottom of the case had been knocked out, the bottles emptied of their contents, filled with water, and then corked up again. It only shows how little afraid the looters were of being disturbed, and the leisurely way they were able to carry out their robbery.

We left De Aar at two o'clock on the afternoon of Monday, January 22, for Prieska, which is about 130 miles distant, our flying column consisting of two companies of mounted infantry, Roberts' Horse, and six guns, three of them belonging to a field battery, and the other three to the Cape Garrison Artillery.

The country between De Aar and Prieska is uninteresting. On account of the thick bush and rocky surface of the ground, we were obliged for the greater part of the march to keep to the road. The whole country bristles with ironstone:

the glare and the heat rising from the ground were tremendous. The second day's march brought us to Britstown, which is rather a pretty village, but had the unenviable reputation of being a strong rebel centre; however, we managed to get a tub and a fairly good dinner at the hotel.

Next day we camped at Houwater on one of Mr Rhodes's farms, and saw what perseverance and enterprise could accomplish in such a barren-looking spot. A perfect system of irrigation, which is necessary to successful farming in South Africa, had been carried out all over this huge farm. An immense reservoir had been constructed by damming the valley between two small kopjes, through which there ran a stream called the Ongers River. Later, I believe, this farm was raided by the Boers.

At the side of the road about ten miles from Houwater we came upon a curious little post-box, intended no doubt for the convenience of farms in the neighbourhood; but as far as the naked eye could see there was only the open veldt—not a building of any kind in sight anywhere.

On the Saturday we had the welcome sight of a fringe of green, which was the trees outlining the Orange River; at about four that afternoon we reached Prieska, and found camped there a company of the New Zealand Mounted Rifles. We were pointed out some distant hills, where there was a rebel laager, across the river; but, as the river was too swollen to cross, we and the enemy

Schilderspan post-box.

could have done no more than glare at each other from opposite banks.

Prieska itself is a miserable village, the river being its one attraction. We were entertained that night at an outdoor smoking-concert got up by the residents of the town, and spent quite a jovial evening; a most patriotic song was sung by some children armed with little Union Jacks, which created great enthusiasm, the whole audience afterwards joining heartily in "God save the Queen!"

On the following day, Sunday, we were astonished by a command to leave that night for the Orange River station. The marching orders were to be kept perfectly secret: so the Prieska people, who had no inkling of our sudden departure, must have been somewhat surprised, on waking up next morning, to find our camp deserted. This sudden desertion of Prieska also must have come very hard on the loyalists, who, emboldened by our presence, gave expression to their pent-up feelings; and no doubt they had a bad time when we left. The night was dark, and a cold mist hung over the veldt, as, at one in the morning, we left our camp and marched to Klip Drift, about twenty-five miles off. Three more marches brought us to Hope Town, which is only about twelve miles from Orange River station, where we marched in early next morning, having covered about 100 miles since leaving Prieska; our longest march was thirty-five miles. Opposite is the left-hand corner of the Kimberley map issued to us, and not, as you might suppose, a portion of a map of Ireland; perhaps the so-called rebel Irish Brigade recruited in this district! (Should I explain, to prevent wounding the feelings of the loyal farmers in this district, that I don't mean this seriously?)

Next day, February 3, we were once more on the move, and marched to Witte Puts station, which is fourteen miles north on the Kimberley line, passing on the way many troops moving

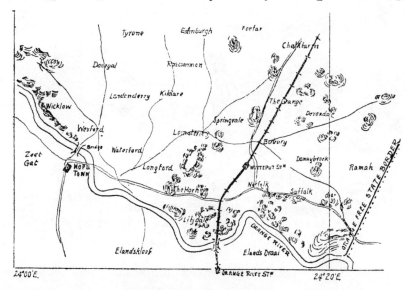

Section of map of Kimberley.

forward. From there we were sent off the following morning to Richmond Farm, with a view, we understood, to punishing the Douglas rebels, who were again, after Colonel Pilcher's successful action a few weeks before, beginning to be troublesome.

We were joined here by Colonel Pilcher and his mounted infantry, and P Battery R.H.A., under Major Sir Godfrey Thomas. Colonel Broad-wood arrived to take command of the column. We had two days' rest while waiting for the remainder of the column to concentrate. On the 6th we made a night march with the object of trying to surprise the rebels who were laagered

The author's shelter at Richmond.

outside Douglas; however, they had left in a hurry, and, we heard, had run up against General Sir Hector Macdonald at Koodoes Berg Drift. We know now that this demonstration on Cronje's left flank was done by Lord Roberts with the view of deceiving the former as to his real intention of relieving Kimberley through the Orange Free State.

While at Richmond, during the silent blackness of each night we saw the flash of the Kimberley searchlight, darting hither and thither over the heavens like some pent-up spirit vainly seeking a means of escape. One could not watch this quivering light dart upwards from the besieged town without pondering on what the flash would reveal could we but read the signal.

Kaffir hut at Richmond.

After returning from Douglas we had another rest, for one day, and then started off to join General French's division, which, we heard, was concentrating at Ramdam for an important move in connection with the relief of Kimberley. The thirty-four miles from Richmond to Ramdam we covered in two marches, stopping at Belmont on the way.

Perhaps this will convey some idea of the numerous kopjes at Belmont, where Lord Methuen had a successful engagement on November 23. The highest kopje is Kaffir Kop; it was here, we were told, that the Guards lost so heavily.

Belmont.

While passing through the kopjes we came across abundant evidence of fighting there, in the quantity of brown-paper wrappings for mauser ammunition which were thickly strewn about the veldt.

Eight miles from Belmont we crossed the Orange Free State border, and immediately struck the old camping-ground of a Boer commando. There was no sign of any hurried departure here, in which respect the place was different from the camping-grounds we subsequently came across after the relief of Kimberley; the only evidences of the place having been a camp were a few sardine tins and bits of old skins scattered about, and the patches of veldt worn bare where the Boer tents had been left undisturbed so long.

Overleaf is a sketch of a match-box I picked up —not a very artistic production, but depicting a battle as the Boer would wish it — I don't say that we should not also, had we the choice : plenty of cannon and a frowning kopje awaiting the attackers to storm.

We reached Ramdam on the afternoon of the 11th, to find the whole of the remainder of General French's division already concentrated there, and just in time to take part in the dash for Kimberley, as at 2 a.m. next morning we were off; before this we had covered over three hundred miles since leaving De Aar on January 22. There was not much rest at Ramdam : we had to draw several days' supplies for the men and horses and have everything ready for the early start on the morrow.

General French's division was made up of three

brigades of cavalry—the 1st Brigade commanded
by Colonel Porter, the 2nd Brigade by Colonel
Broadwood, the 3rd Brigade by Colonel Gordon;
six batteries of Royal Horse Artillery; and a
mounted infantry brigade, commanded by Colonel
Alderson, composed of the 1st Mounted Infantry

Commando match-box.

Regiment, Roberts' Horse, the New Zealand
Mounted Rifles, Australian Mounted Infantry, and
Rimmington's Guides, unattached. The total
number of men was about 5000.

At two on the morning of February 12 we
moved off, the 2nd Brigade on the right, the
1st Brigade in the centre, and the 3rd Brigade on

the left; the mounted infantry were with the 1st
Brigade.   It was moonlight when we started; but
the moon soon disappeared, and left us to feel our
way in the dark; the rumble of the gun-wheels,
and shadowy forms of horsemen in one's immediate
front, every now and again swaying outwards as
" Ware hole!" was passed back, were the only
evidences to be heard or seen of this huge column
advancing.   At daybreak our patrols came in
contact with the enemy in the neighbourhood
of Waterval Drift.   A battery of horse artillery
was immediately ordered up to shell the Boer
position; the two companies of the 1st Mounted
Infantry Regiment, which I was temporarily
commanding, moving up with them as escort.
Galloping ahead and then wheeling sharply to
the left under cover of a low kopje, the guns
unlimbered and came into action.   Their shells
whistled over our heads, and grew fainter and
fainter until, almost dying away in the distance
with a sharp report, like a rocket exploding, they
burst beautifully over the crest of the kopjes
held by the enemy, and very soon we saw the
Boers moving off up the river on the far side.

The following sketch will give some idea of the
ugly nature of the country north of Waterval Drift.

The kopjes marked A were held by the 6th Inniskilling Dragoons. Prince Alexander of Teck brought a message asking me to reinforce them if I could, and while returning came under a very hot fire, but got through untouched. The two companies 1st Mounted Infantry held the kopjes B and C. Our shells can be seen bursting over

Country near Waterval Drift.

the Boers, who were moving up the stream with the intention, no doubt, of holding De Kiel's Drift before we could reach it.

Meanwhile the 1st Brigade and remainder of the mounted infantry moved off in a south-easterly direction, and, forestalling the Boers, captured De Kiel's Drift with but slight opposition. In securing this, however, Captain Majendie of the Rifle Brigade, commanding Roberts' Horse, was mortally wounded. He was carried into a farmhouse on the near side of the drift, and died next morning.

We eventually all crossed the river at this drift, and bivouacked on the right bank; but it was not till late that night that our transport crossed. It had been a scorching hot day, and for the first time I realised what it was to have one's lips and tongue so parched and swollen with thirst that one could hardly speak. While waiting for the transport to arrive we had a bath in the water of the Riet, sinking knee-deep in the mud before we could reach the stream. Impatiently we waited our waggons, not having had anything to eat, save the little biscuit we carried in our haver-sacks, since our breakfast at one o'clock that morning. When they did at length arrive, we speedily sat down to a dinner, and appreciated our scant fare as we had never done before. Although it had been a long and tiring day, we had not covered more than sixteen miles.

Next morning we formed up in line of brigade masses—the mounted infantry with Colonel Broad-wood's 2nd Brigade. For the first time we saw what an imposing sight—how large and business-like—this force was. Lord Roberts and his staff, who had ridden into camp that morning, witnessed our departure as we moved off amid clouds of dust. We now came into the fine rolling grassy

plains of the Free State, an ideal country for a large
mounted force. Our advance was not interrupted
until the afternoon, when our right flank encountered a good deal of opposition, and our guns
immediately came into action. A fierce veldt fire
was raging on our left; fanned by the wind from
that direction, it was steadily bearing down on to
us, who were between it and the guns in action
on our right. Caught between these two fires,
we had, as may be imagined, an exciting gallop to
get through.

Our objective was to reach and secure a passage
over the Modder. This had to be done, as the river
was our only available water-supply. The Modder
at this part bristles with drifts; but I must leave
it to others to describe the manner in which
General French deceived the Boers into thinking
that we were making for one or other of the drifts,
except the two we eventually did secure. At the
time, of course, we had no knowledge of how this
was being effected.

A dark line stretching across the withered grass
of the veldt, at first indistinct but gradually becom-
ing more and more pronounced as we rode on, gave
us the first welcome news that we were nearing the
river. Soon the green of the trees fringing the

4   The end of the day

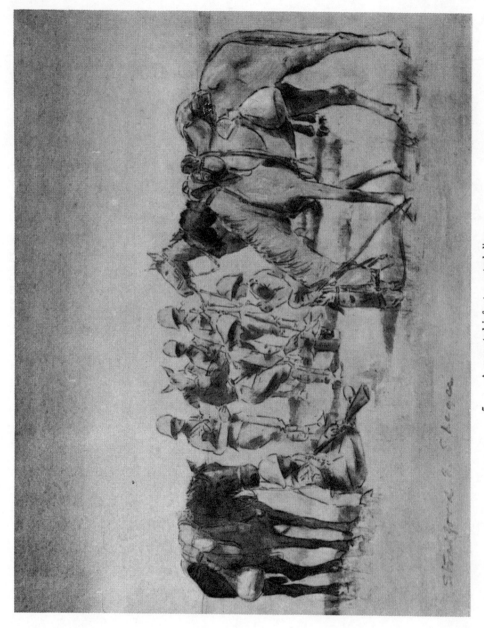

5   A mounted infantry patrol dinner

banks of the Modder was plainly discernible.   As
we came up accompanying the horse artillery, we
could see the tents of a Boer laager across the
river at Klip Drift.   The guns immediately unlimbered and searched the trees lining the river bank

Between two fires.

with shrapnel; and, under cover of their fire, the
cavalry of the 2nd Brigade forced the drift, following the retreating Boers for two miles on the
opposite side.   Leaving the guns, we followed, and
were well rewarded for crossing the river, as, though
I saw only one Boer, who was running towards
us waving his hands in great anxiety to show
that he wished to surrender, we came across an

abundance of oat-hay and the most excellent water at a farm. I don't recollect ever meeting with such a pure spring again in the whole country. We re-crossed the river and bivouacked on the left bank, while the cavalry remained on the right bank, having covered about thirty miles during the day.

On the 14th we were obliged to halt to enable General Kelly-Kenny's division to arrive and hold the drifts. The only excitement during the day was the firing of a few shells from a long-range gun into our camp, and the appearance of some Boers on the opposite bank of the river to the east of our bivouac. They were shelled by us and easily driven off. I believe all they were attempting to do was to rescue the contents of some waggons which they had abandoned on our appearance the day before.

On the morning of the 15th we crossed the Modder, and formed up with the Cavalry Division on the right bank. There was not the slightest sign of hurry or excitement, nothing to show that an adventurous day was in front of us. However, we all knew it full well—Kimberley had to be relieved that day at all costs. The enforced halt on the previous day had given the Boers ample opportunity to hurry up reinforcements, and to make preparations to bar our advance, and we did not know how fully they had taken advantage of this.

For the better explanation of the day's work, I have drawn a rough plan of the ground, taken from my Kimberley map. The whole division was

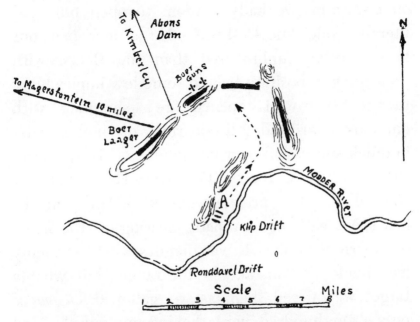

Plan showing General French's operations on February 15.

formed up in column of brigade masses at the point marked A, Colonel Gordon's brigade being in front, ready to bear the brunt of the fighting; we were in rear. It was not until the morning was well advanced that we got the order to move, and we had covered but a short distance when the

signal to trot and then canter was given; the guns
of the 1st Brigade, which were just in front of
us, at the same time dashed into position on the
extreme end of the low-lying kopje on our left.
Hemmed in as we were by this ridge and the river
on our right, we had no room to open out, and
literally rode knee-to-knee. No sooner had our
horse artillery unlimbered than the Boers, with
their guns in position behind some low kopjes lying
to the north-west, opened fire; shrapnel, with
ominous report and tell-tale rings of smoke, burst
in quick succession over our gunners. It was here
that poor little Carbett of G Battery Horse Artillery
was killed. The previous day, with two guns, he
had spent with my company clearing off the Boers
on our right flank. It was manifest that the enemy
had made no mistake in the range; but what a
target we offered them as we galloped *en masse*
only a few hundred yards behind our guns! Had
they known it, surely they must have devoted a
shell or two to us.

In the midst of the clattering of hoofs and dust,
my horse, stumbling in a hole, came down, and I
found myself under a *mêlée* of plunging horses. It
was the work of a few seconds only to remount
and gallop into my place, and now the finest sight

of the whole war burst on our view. We were
following the bend of the river and heading
straight for the kopjes shown on the right of
the sketch plan, which ran north and south and
at right angles to those on our left; the latter,
however, came to an abrupt end, and showed
us a plain about three or four thousand yards
across, extending to the ridge behind which the
Boers had their guns. From the kopjes shown
on the right of the sketch plan, the Boers had
opened a brisk fire on our cavalry advanced guard.
The Boer position was unmasked, and we seemed
in a tight corner, with the river hemming us in on
the right, Boer guns on our left, and to our front a
line of kopjes held by the enemy, who were also
extended across the intervening plain. In the
sketch the Boer position is shown by a thick
line, the direction of our advance and our cavalry
charge by the dotted lines with arrow heads.

There was not the slightest pause, and, apparently
without a moment's hesitation, General French
gave his orders. Detaching one cavalry regiment
to turn the kopjes to our front under cover of the
guns of the 2nd Brigade, he ordered Colonel
Gordon's brigade to charge straight up the valley
into the very mouths, it seemed, of the Boer guns,

and the other brigades to conform to the movement. Each successive line as it came to the open ground circled round, and, opening out, thundered up the plain in a cloud of dust. We each followed in turn; and as we passed over the ground, beyond a few dead and wounded horses and wounded men, there was nothing to show that a cavalry charge had taken place. The Boers, yielding, galloped off, and with the utmost haste got their guns away.

General French had broken through the Boer position, and the relief of Kimberley was assured.

Calmly looking back on the day, one can realise how anxiously General French must have watched that leading brigade's charge. The sword and lance have been very severely criticised; but it was these " obsolete and absurd weapons," as they have been called, that won the day. The moral effect of a charge of lancers or dragoons, armed with their proper weapons, is a force to be reckoned with, not to be lightly cast aside.

Praise for an M, Official

We made a short halt at Abon's Dam for water, and then pushed on, catching the first sight of Kimberley between three and four in the afternoon, a long line of tall chimneys and mining shafts standing out black against the sparkling of the many corrugated iron roofs.

Yet another incident awaited us before we reached our destination. We were halted for a few moments opposite Olifant's laager, a fact which we speedily found out. As a finale to their retirement, the Boers put five shells into our brigade. The first came short; the second went over our heads; but the remaining three fell immediately between my regiment and the New Zealand Mounted Rifles, which was exactly the centre of the target we offered them. A tablecloth might have almost covered the spot where these three shells fell. One plunged into the ground directly under my farrier-sergeant's horse, another under one of my subaltern's, and the third between the doctor of the New Zealanders and myself, almost grazing my horse's neck. A shell coming directly towards you one hears for a long distance; the hissing, as it cleaves its way through the air, growing louder and louder until with a thud it strikes the ground, throwing up a cloud of dust and earth.

Luckily for us, the shells went to ground without
exploding: the surface being soft, they simply
sank in. We afterwards visited this laager, and
found tents standing, with many other evidences
of a very rapid departure.

Tent left at Olifant's laager.

The sun had set before we passed the first mines
outside Beaconsfield. One or two men rode out to
meet us, and a few Kaffir boys waved their hats as
we passed; but otherwise it looked as if we had
relieved a deserted town. I am unable to describe

the actual entry of General French into the town,
as I did not see it; but from all accounts he
seems to have had a very enthusiastic welcome.
It was dark before we had watered our horses and
bivouacked at Blankensberg's Vlei, after a march
of close on thirty miles.

Early the next morning we were saddled up
and soon on the move again, taking part in the
disappointing fight at Dronfield. We occupied
the ridges just vacated by the Boers, and had
plenty of opportunities of seeing how securely they
had entrenched themselves. From here I made
the sketch of Kimberley, the frontispiece to this
chapter.

Returning to Kimberley, I let my horse guide
us to our bivouac. What a marvellous bump of
locality a horse must have! In and out of the
various bluestone-gravel heaps, all exactly alike,
and through the different camps, mine threaded his
way, leading us without the slightest hesitation
direct to ours. Not having had leisure to shave for
several days, I was pluming myself on the good
time I should have when I got in that evening;
but of course the unexpected happened. When
we did reach our camp I found that in our absence
my led pony, which had been saddled up in the

morning, had broken loose ; when she was recovered by my servant, my saddle-bags had been ripped open and everything that they contained looted—razors, change of underwear, and even my papers and sketch-book. Thus I lost the majority of my Prieska sketches. Thinking of this, I can't say that I have the kindliest recollection of my welcome to Kimberley.

The utility of this ride from a strategical point of view has been severely criticised, and carping critics have maintained that the advantages gained by relieving Kimberley in this manner in no way compensated for the waste of horseflesh involved. These critics, I fancy, lose sight of one important consideration. It is that by General French reaching Kimberley not only was the town relieved, but also only one avenue of escape to Bloemfontein was left open to Cronje, and this resulted in his complete capture at Paardeberg. That Cronje saw the importance of our move may be gathered from the rapid but ineffectual attempt he made to escape from the trap laid for him. Moreover, the moral effect on the Boers of Cronje's surrender may be gauged by their headlong flight before our advance. They abandoned Bloemfontein with but a feeble show of resistance, and their strongly

6   The bed of the river at Paardeberg

entrenched position at Kroonstad practically without firing a shot, allowing us to cross the Vaal in the same way. It was only at Klipriversberg that they began to recover, and that any serious attempt at a stand was made. Their rally there, however, was momentary. They again fled before our advance from Johannesburg to Pretoria, and there seems little doubt but that the war would have been brought to a rapid close after the fall of the capital had it not been for the successful attacks De Wet made on our lines of communication in rear. This counteracted Paardeberg, buoyed up the disheartened burghers with renewed hopes of success, and induced them to continue the struggle.

Deducing this indirect result of French's ride to Kimberley, one cannot look upon it otherwise than as a fine achievement and a grand success.

TOMMY: SOME ANECDOTES

TOMMY: SOME ANECDOTES

No reminiscences or impressions of the Boer War, however trifling, would be complete without some tribute to Tommy. He has had many champions; but he has also had his traducers. I think that it has very clearly been proved that these last were either slandering intentionally for a particular purpose, or else were painfully ignorant.

There could be no better judge of the stuff Tommy is made of than our own medical officers. " I know that footslogging T. A. is a hero," said one whose opinion is worth having; and we can all echo the words without reserve.

I always had a high opinion of Tommy, and have often thought that there was not a soldier of any other country who could possibly surpass or even equal him. This was my firm conviction, formed before I had seen him on service; and now, after having seen him under every condition imaginable, both in disaster and in victory, my opinion has undergone no change—except to become strengthened.

Shortly after returning home I was astonished to see a statement, made, as far as I recollect, by a man in the service, to the effect that no one was more surprised at the bravery and endurance of his men than the officer who had known them only in peace time. I cannot imagine anything more erroneous or more at variance with the truth. No one who has the slightest insight into human nature, or has studied his men in peace time, could ever have been guilty of such an error of judgment. We could not help feeling gratified, but never surprised, that Tommy came up to our preconceived ideal of him. I do not speak from knowledge of the men of my own regiment exclusively. The company which I trained before the war and commanded in South Africa was a composite one made up from Irish, English, and Welsh regiments. It would be invidious to pick out any regiment or nationality. Each has its own characteristics; but true blood runs in them all, and all are chivalrous and gallant.

Tommy is seen at his best when there is hard work to be done. Though he may growl in his own peculiar way when fatigues are heavy in the course of the ordinary barrack routine, never a grumble comes from the same man on service, albeit he is on half rations and with but one blanket to cover him. It is no exaggeration to say that I never heard a single man complain during the whole time I was in South Africa, even though all the troops had been soaking-wet through and practically living on a couple of biscuits for days at a time, chilled to the bone and without fuel or time enough to cook their rations of trek-ox. Nay: the damper their condition the cheerier they seemed to get. The wetter the night the happier the song. Tommy always sings when it is wet. Walk through any camp when the rain is coming down in torrents, when the camp is a sea of mud, when there is not an inch of dry canvas to be found anywhere, and every tent is leaking,—you will hear nothing but good-natured banter, cracking of jokes, and singing—a good rollicking song too, with a lusty chorus.

Identically the same as these were the men who slept for months in the open veldt—my own men slept in the open from January 22 until October 28, with the exception of one week under canvas—with no other covering than a pair of blankets, often with no more than one, when the bitterly cold winter's rain and the intense frost had turned the veldt into a marsh by day and into a sheet of ice by night. How they withstood it, heaven only knows; but there is

A wet day at Koedoesrand.

nothing if not a stout heart underneath Tommy's veldt-stained clothes.

It is true they had fine examples set them. Our own Brigadier, Colonel Alderson, I have seen night after night, merely wrapped up in his blankets and waterproof sheet, lying in the open veldt, which the heavy rains had turned into a swamp.

leadership

I know nothing more trying than to be night after night unable to sleep owing to the cold: could anything have been nobler than Tommy's behaviour amid these circumstances? Frequently our transport did not reach us until late at night. At such times it went to my heart to have to go round before marching off in the morning and order a man's blanket here and a rug there to be taken off a pony, knowing full well that probably we should not see our waggons until the night was well advanced, and (in the winter and in high country such as the Gatsrand) with a heavy frost holding everything in its firm grip, the more keenly felt because of the violent change from the intense heat of the day.

The instinct of sport is born and bred in Tommy: he must always be in at the death: he is never too done up to go on as long as sport is forward. I have had men, who for some reason or other had been ordered by our medical officer to be left behind, coming to me with tears in their eyes begging me to allow them to go on with the column.

Tommy certainly has a complex character. When one might naturally expect him to become serious, the spirit of comedy awakes within him. I have seen men roaring with laughter at a helmet

being knocked off by a pom-pom shell at a time
when these spiteful little missiles were playing
through our ranks. I must say that the astonished
look of the owner of the helmet, as he grabbed at
his head to see that it was all there, was irresistibly
comic—though this, I fancy, was a little bit of
acting on his part.

An amusing incident occurred when our pom-
pom, commanded by Captain De Winton, R.A.,
was under a perfect blizzard of shells at Klipriversberg. There were half a dozen Boer guns doing
their best to silence this one little pom-pom.
When the fusillade began the gunners were
boiling water for their breakfast; but as the
Boer shells began dropping all round the fire,
they were obliged to seek cover near the gun.
One of the men, who with an anxious eye had
been for some time fixedly staring at the fire,
suddenly remarked, " Begorra, the kettle is after
bilin' over," darted out and brought it safely
in, and, regardless of shells or anything else, set
to making the tea.

There are times when Tommy's callousness
comes from not quite realising the danger he is in.
One of our men had been intently watching the
sand spurting up round him for some time, and

scratching his head to try and think what sort of animals were causing this disturbance, when all of a sudden he made the brilliant discovery what these might be. " Be gob, Pat, is them bullets ? " he asked of his nearest comrade.

This incident recalls to my mind another told me by a subaltern of my regiment. He saw one of his men creeping up to him, and called out to know what was the matter. " Please, sorr, Private Flanagan is after being hit in the fut and is bawlin' an' dancin' about an' dhrawin' all the fire on us. What shall we do ? "

Tommy, if not, strictly speaking, witty, always has a ready answer. It is worth hearing two or three of them having a sparring match, as they fling good-humoured retorts at one another. One needs to be a first-rate mimic to repeat their droll sayings, which lose a great deal without the accompaniment of voice and gesture. The following little passage was overheard one evening when we were returning to camp after rather a hot engagement. " What was it loike, Mike ? Plenty of ant-heaps, I suppose ? " " Ant-heaps ! there warn't enough of them for the blooming hofficer ! "

I will give one little incident that happened after

a long and hard day—every one of us could give similar incidents by the score. I saw my servant approaching ; evidently he was carrying something precious in his haversack. "I got this for you from an old Boer farmer, sorr." "What is it, Murphy?" "Ah, it is nothing much—only a bit of fresh butter and a couple of eggs, sorr. The old Boer said he was after getting six shillings a dozen for them eggs in Bloomfontine, and I was lucky to get them at all." "Have you got any for yourself, Murphy?" "Ah, sure I'm all right." After a while I took a quiet stroll round to see what the "all right" was, and found just what I expected— no eggs or butter, but the hard, dry ration biscuits and a small piece of fresh, tough, tasteless meat which was slowly cooking in his mess-tin.

If you can form any idea what these small luxuries would have been to Tommy at that time —and I doubt whether you can, unless you happen to know the meaning of a dinner of dry ration biscuit and trek-ox—you will be able to realise what a generous heart throbs under that mud-stained khaki. Had there been any Boer refugee women and children in camp, without a moment's hesitation he would have given up his small meat ration as well, did he think they required it.

It was against such men as these that the foul charges made on the Continent found a ready echo from many self-righteous humbugs at home.

There is one thing which above everything else serves to put Tommy in a false light; and that is due to his peculiar ideas on the subject of letter-writing.   He does not often write letters; but when the pen is taken up it means business.   In order to give a vivid account of his doings, he thinks it necessary to draw on his fertile brain for the material; and crammed into one letter we get the concentrated essence of many valiant deeds. The Guardsman who in writing home said that, having found it took half an hour to extract his bayonet from a victim, he had decided to leave his rifle and bayonet in the next, and thus lost four rifles in one day, is a good example of what I mean.   Don't judge Tommy from letters such as these.   Believe me, his letters belie him.   Tommy is no braggart at heart, and has the most chivalrous regard for a fallen foe.   Could anything have shown the truth of this more forcibly than his behaviour on our entry into Bloemfontein, Kroonstad, and Pretoria?   There were many ludicrous sights during those times; but never once did I hear Tommy make fun of the Boers then.   They were a beaten foe, and as such he treated them with honour and respect ; and, mind you, it was his own chivalrous instinct that prompted him to act as he did—it was never necessary to issue any orders on the subject. Walk beside any regiment at home during peace manœuvres, and you will hear the troops laughing and cracking jokes at anybody or anything that appeals to their keen sense of humour. These same men in face of their beaten enemy, who often presented sights far more laughable than anything they had seen before, never dreamt of doing aught else than pass them in chivalrous silence. This courteous, gentlemanly treatment was in many instances received with utter *sang-froid* and ingratitude. It may have been due to misunderstanding ; but I am inclined to think not. It made my blood boil to see men who had surrendered at Bloemfontein, and were magnanimously allowed to roam about the town at their own sweet will, spitting on the ground as our soldiers passed them. The impudence was unmistakable ; but the only possible answer was either to take absolutely no notice or else administer a sound thrashing on the spot, and the former course was the only one open to us.

The Boer also, judging from the number of such

letters that we found lying at deserted farms and torn up on old sites of laagers, was fond of describing his adventures. De Rougemont even might have been staggered by some of them. As often as not these letters were written in good English. My only regret is that I could not keep some of them. The following is an extract from an epistle picked up by one of my men at a deserted farm: —"This morning I saw Lord Salisbury lying dead. I only just missed getting his watch and chain, but I got his sword. Koetzee got the watch before I could grab it, but I hope to get another soon."

We must not judge the Boer from his letters any more than our own Tommy ; but a history of the war as told in these letters could not fail to be entertaining. Tommy, among many other excellent attributes, has a most forgiving and good-natured character. He never showed the slightest resentment towards the Boers, but at once met them on a footing of comradeship. After heartily shaking hands with the surrendered burgher, out came the friendly pipe, and, passing round his little store of precious tobacco, before many minutes were over he would raise a laugh out of the most taciturn or crestfallen among the burghers. Not that many of them seemed very down on their luck. As a rule they professed to be exceedingly glad at having been captured; at any rate, after a few minutes in Tommy's company they certainly gave one that impression.

THE SIEGE OF KIMBERLEY

8   A corner of Cronje's laager at Paardeberg

9   An ox convoy

THE SIEGE OF KIMBERLEY

THE siege of Kimberley will always remain one of
the most interesting episodes of the war, owing to
the fact that Colonel Kekewich had to depend
mainly upon its citizen garrison to defend the town.
The mere handful of regulars at his disposal would
have been powerless without aid. Having formed
one of the relief party, I am of course without
any personal reminiscences of this interesting
siege.   I am fortunate, however, in being permitted to give an interesting excerpt from a
letter relating the experiences of an old school-
friend who as one of the Town Guard took part
in its defence :—

"In accordance with my promise, I am now
going to jot down a few notes about the siege of
Kimberley. Little did we think in the old days at
school, when trying to instil what drill we knew
into our fellow-cadets, that it was a prelude to

something more serious, and that one of us would welcome the other in the guise of a reliever.

" Towards the middle of 1899 we were, of course, all discussing the possibilities of war; but the first token of its probability was a visit one Sunday from three officers—Colonel Trotter, R.A., now on the headquarters staff, Major Scott-Turner of the Black Watch, and Lieutenant (now Captain) MacInnes, R.E.—who after chatting some while asked permission to look at the gardens and paddocks round our house. This was part of a minute survey which they were making with a view to a possible defence of the town.

" The first-named did not remain long at Kimberley; but the two others were with us throughout the siege, the former organising and acquiring information as to resources, and the latter surveying and planning redoubts. As you must have noted, Kimberley lends itself very readily to fortification against both shell and rifle fire. There are no commanding heights: the country is open, and the countless heaps of *débris* require the lightest of spade work to be converted into redoubts, with excellent stopping properties and no danger from splinters.

" Colonel Kekewich of the Loyal North Lancashire Regiment came up from Cape Town about the middle of September.   This completed the staff of imperial officers, consisting of Major Scott-Turner, Royal Highlanders, staff officer ; Captain O'Meara, R.E., intelligence officer; and Lieutenant MacInnes, R.E., with Colonel Kekewich in command.   A week later half the Loyal North Lancashire Regiment arrived, a well-set-up body of men, who shot well, and in their first affair at Dronfield on October 24, well handled by Major (now Lieutenant-Colonel) Murray, negotiating a kopje in most excellent style, killed the Boer leader, and turned a somewhat anxious affair into a victory.

"They were the first body of regulars who had been stationed in Kimberley for about ten years, and were received with great enthusiasm.   There also arrived a company of garrison artillery under Major Chamier, who brought six seven-pounder mountain-battery guns.   These, with the battery of seven-pounder muzzle-loading guns of the local field battery, constituted our artillery resources. Why a couple of 6-inch guns were not spared us from Simon's Bay I have hitherto failed to grasp.

"The Volunteers were now called out ; and thus, fortunately, Major Chamier had a short time in which to train his field battery, which, under

Major May, a De Beers' employé who took command of it, had been in a very parlous condition; this was owing, no doubt, to the way in which the Colonial authorities neglected it.

"When I returned to Kimberley on the night of October 14, after an absence of three weeks, I found that a ring of redoubts, connected by mimosa and wire entanglements, had sprung up about the hitherto peaceful town, under the ægis of Lieutenant MacInnes, of the Royal Engineers, assisted by Lieutenant M'Clintock, of the same corps, and a section of sappers. These works were made under the direction of the sappers by a body of natives lent by the De Beers Company.

"Major Scott-Turner had planned a Town Guard, whose formation the High Commissioner had shortly before sanctioned. This body, then about 1200 strong, rose in numbers as soon as war was actually declared, and ultimately attained a strength of about 2700. The Volunteers numbered about 600; and the Cape Police, by subsequent acquisitions from those stationed along the railway and from outlying stations, eventually rose to about 400.

"In this connection may be mentioned the feat of Major Berrange, of the Cape Police, who

THE SIEGE OF KIMBERLEY

brought in his men all the way from Upington, which is situated about 300 miles west of Kimberley on the Orange River; he not only accomplished this march in an incredibly short time, but also worked his way into Kimberley through the Boer lines. This was only one of many similar performances by this magnificent corps, who were composed of Colonials, Dutchmen, and public-school boys—forming the ideal corps for the country.

"Our garrison thus merely totalled about 3700 men, with a stiffening of only 500 regulars; and our artillery resources consisted of only a scanty supply of ammunition and muzzle-loading seven-pounders—fourteen in number. These were made up as follows:—the 23rd Company Royal Garrison Artillery, one battery Diamond Fields Artillery, and two old Cape Police guns; the range of the latter was no more than that of the mauser rifle. With this body we had to hold a perimeter of close on ten miles.

"With regard to food supplies, I think I am correct in saying that the authorities never put a biscuit into the place. Major Scott-Turner interviewed the biggest firms, who undertook to get in stocks to last them for three months. Offers, I believe, were made to increase these stocks if the

Imperial Government guaranteed the price; but these offers were declined.

"With regard to our water supply, it must be remembered that the reservoir is not of any great capacity, holding, as it does, not more than thirty days' supply, and is fed from the Vaal River, some sixteen or seventeen miles away.

"Fortunately, when the Boers cut the pipes, which they promptly did, the De Beers Company were able to couple up the pumping gear at Wesselton (Premier mine), and a supply of good water was ensured so long as our fuel lasted. This important point in the defences, though outside our perimeter, was held by Captain O'Brien of the North Lancashires, with a company of his men, two guns of the Royal Garrison Artillery, and the employés of the mine.

"When the siege began, Major Scott-Turner was staff officer; but shortly after, with the local rank of Lieutenant-Colonel, he took command of the Mounted Corps, comprising the Cape Police, Diamond Fields Horse, Loyal North Lancashire Regiment, Mounted Infantry, and Kimberley Light Horse. His place as staff officer was taken by Lieutenant MacInnes, R.E. Popular socially, a tremendous worker in office, where his position as a

buffer between the officer commanding the forces
and the importunate civilian must have been most
wearing, yet ever alert, especially at dawn, when
he might be found riding round the weakest spots
of our defence on the *qui vive* for an attack, this

Ammunition mule.

smart young officer seemed to change during these
four months from a smiling youth to an anxious
man; and has to my mind received most inade-
quate recognition for great services. Kimberley
will ever hold him in kindly remembrance.

" The history of the siege may be said to divide itself into two parts, the active and the passive, much as that of Methuen's force does.

" During the former, the mounted corps under the heroic Scott-Turner made several sorties, one of which on the Saturday previous to the battle of Modder River was most successful, thirty-five

Cattle-guarding.

prisoners being taken. We paid heavily for these sorties, losing between thirty and forty killed and seventy wounded.

" After the death of the gallant Scott-Turner, who fell with twenty-one others while engaged in preventing the Boers in our neighbourhood from sending reinforcements to Modder River when the battle of that name was in progress, the mounted men, barring one or two slight affairs in which their losses were trifling, confined their operations

to the irksome but necessary work of cattle-guarding. Though constantly sniped at, I think I am
correct in saying, they never lost a man killed at
this work, so that the Boer shooting at long ranges
does not appear to have been always good.

"The battle of Magersfontein, fought on
December 11, is a day we in Kimberley shall
never forget. At about four in the morning the
welcome booming of distant artillery was heard;
and a message from Colonel Kekewich, who was
watching from the 'Conning Tower,' told us that
our shells could be seen bursting upon the crests
of the hills occupied by Cronje.

"On proceeding to the ridge near the race-
course one could plainly see the hills in the direction of the Modder River, belching smoke. It was
quite easy to discriminate between the burst of our
shells and the puff from the Boer guns replying.
Subsequently it was a recognised pastime to go to
this ridge on the chance of seeing a bombardment
in progress, and once I had the pleasure of seeing
a Boer magazine blow up.

"Methuen's war balloon could also be detected
like a minute black pear in the sky. For hours
the incessant roar continued, till one felt quite
sorry for the foe, whom we pictured being blown

off the face of the earth by this terrific fire; and
we all thought that by night we should be clasping
some of the relieving force by the hand. But
it was not to be.   Those who could understand the
heliograph might have
read the insolent mes-
sage from the Boers
about mid-day: 'We
have knocked your
precious relief column
to blazes.'

" A few days went by,
and we heard nothing,

Captive war balloon.

though I may mention, as an instance of how
information gets about where there are natives to
give it, that one of them told me he had heard that
our force had got into trouble through barbed wire;
and it was only when a Cape Town newspaper got
in that we realised what had happened.

" In anticipation of Methuen's entrance, a step had been taken which roused great indignation. This was the preparation of a census of the inhabitants, with a note in the case of non-com-

Getting information from natives.

batants, as to the place they would elect to reside in outside Kimberley; it being the intention of the military authorities to remove all non-combatants to the coast, provision the town, and then cease to hold the railway.

" One can understand the indignation aroused

when one considers that hundreds of women and
children, of little or no means, would naturally feel
alarmed at the prospect of going, *sans* husbands,
fathers, or brothers, to the coast-towns already
overcrowded by refugees from the Transvaal and
the Free State, not knowing what bad news they
might hear from day to day of those they had
left behind.

" Had the necessity arisen for the carrying out
of this project, it would have meant not only the
banishment of these people from their homes, but
also absolute bankruptcy and ruin to many a
struggling shopkeeper.

" Methuen, however, failed to come in, and the
necessity for the enforced exodus of these people
did not arise. The information acquired by the
census nevertheless became useful, for Colonel
Kekewich was not confronted with the problem
of feeding. his large population on a wholly pro-
blematical basis.

" At first the only restriction in the way of
supplies was an order fixing the allowance of meat
at 1 lb. a day for each adult and $\frac{1}{4}$-lb. for each child.
There was no check, however, on the butchers, so
that this order was more or less of a dead letter.
Very soon it became necessary to adopt more

10   A Tonga

11 **A transport driver**

stringent regulations, owing to the sudden rise in the price of provisions to such an enormous extent that starvation confronted many people who, having run through their private stock, were unable to pay the exorbitant prices demanded.

" One of those contemptible attempts by certain speculators to make a fortune out of the misfortunes of their fellow-beings, by buying up all the available supplies of certain articles and thus getting a monopoly, Colonel Kekewich nipped in the bud by publishing a proclamation fixing the price of all the necessaries of life at the figures which were prevalent before the siege.

" When the relief of the town seemed to have been postponed indefinitely, the authorities had the problem of economising the remainder of the available supplies of food, and for this purpose an organisation was formed under the title of 'The Supply Committee'; this body, adopting the municipal arrangement of wards, appointed two or more issuers for each ward.

" An authorised scale of groceries was published, which allowed each European and Colonial one loaf (14 ounces, subsequently reduced to 10 ounces) or 10 ounces of Boer meal or flour, $\frac{1}{2}$ ounce of coffee, $\frac{1}{4}$ ounce of tea, 2 ounces of sugar, 2 ounces

of either samp (crushed maize) or Kaffir corn, and
2 ounces of rice.   All stocks of these articles were
at once taken over from the dealers, who were only

granted quantities sufficient to
carry them on for a week.

"Every householder had to
declare his stock-in-hand, and
was only granted a permit to
purchase fresh supplies when
those declared were estimated
to have been consumed.   Orders to buy were granted once
a week, and no grocer could supply except on
such an order.   These orders were handed over by
the grocer to prove his *bona fides* in getting fresh
stocks from the Committee's depots.

"For Asiatics and Kaffirs a different scale was
drawn up, the former receiving 2 ounces of mealie
meal and 8 ounces of rice, while the latter received
4 ounces of Kaffir corn, 6 ounces of mealie meal,
and 2 ounces of samp.   The allowance of sugar,
coffee, and tea in each case was the same as for
Europeans.

"Similar arrangements were made with regard
to meat, the ultimate scale of which was $\frac{1}{4}$ lb. a
day for non-combatants, and $\frac{1}{2}$ lb. for combatants.

Meat was issued on alternate days to the wards with even numbers and those with odd numbers.

" I need only ask the average English cook how she would like to feed a hungry person for two days on ½ lb. of scraggy horse, during tropical heat, with no cooking-butter or dripping, and but a scanty supply of vegetables, to make you realise one of the trials of the besieged housewife.

" Horseflesh was issued for the first time at the beginning of January; the scale being two-thirds beef and one-third horse. The beef did not last long at this rate, and very soon it came to horse-flesh being issued five days in the week and beef on the remaining two.

" All tinned meats, hams, bacon, jams, and groceries were seized and held as medical comforts, and were only sold on the order of a medical man. It was perhaps providential that they were not all used; for I remember a tin of sardines I was permitted to purchase, when the siege was raised, which suggested a very old vintage; and a prolonged consumption would, I am sure, have necessitated most potent medical comforts.

" Milk was a very scarce article, and the mortality among infants was consequently very high; but every endeavour was made to purchase surplus quantities from the fortunate possessors of cows, and, of course, all tinned milks were seized with the other medical comforts.

"Beyond the daily ration, anything else was

Our meat supply.

considered a luxury, and had to be paid for at a price far in advance of the means of the average person. Potatoes, for example, fetched between 4s. and 5s. a pound, eggs as much as 25s. a dozen, and chickens about 30s. each.

"What with a weekly visit for a grocery order, a daily visit to the baker for bread, a visit every

other day at six in the morning, and a long wait in
a queue, to obtain meat, with probably the following notice forcing itself upon your unwelcome
eyes—

' MEAT SUPPLY.

' The full meat ration of ½ lb. for two days can
be supplied to-day.

' All horse meat.'

—and with the weary task of making this last
palatable, the life of a housewife was not one to
be envied.

" In addition to this, the men were absent all
night and most of the day in the redoubts, so that
there was no one to confront mice, burglars, doubts
and fears. The danger from shell-fire was also
much greater in a house than in a redoubt behind
a soft *débris*-heap, and I think we all look upon
the women as the heroes of Kimberley.

" I may mention that the census revealed a
population of approximately 49,000, over 29,000
being natives. This enormous number were fed for
four months on the supplies held by the merchants
of the place, while the herculean task of organising
the rationing was entrusted to one officer, Captain
Gorle, of the Army Service Corps, and eight of his

men. How he came out of it all a sane man surpasses my comprehension.

"Whether the Boer generals were humane, or whether their ordnance department was feeble, I cannot say; but the bombarding was fitful. Sometimes a week would elapse without a shot being fired; at others it would be confined to a few good-morning and good-night shots — we could generally count on two of the latter. Then, at times they would be quite energetic. This was especially the case after Long Cecil had announced itself, when nine guns barked at us for four days and one night. Shelling at night is not cricket to the mind of the man who has waited through a long summer day for sunset and a comfortable loll in a hammock; 4 a.m. is quite disturbing enough when you are comfortably in bed and not in a dug-out.

"Long Cecil opened fire on January 19, and a few days later the Boers replied by a fierce bombardment of the town. On this day alone close on 500 shells were hurled at us, happily without doing much damage. One poor little girl was killed, and a couple of natives were slightly wounded; these were the total casualties for the day. On the following day the bombardment, though severe, was nothing like as heavy as regards the actual number of shells thrown into the town. The women and children again were the sufferers. The wife and three children of a volunteer in the Town Guard were all seriously injured, one little boy dying the same day from his injuries.

"One of the most miserable aspects of this bombardment was the repeated shelling of funeral processions and actually the cemetery itself, leaving no doubt in anyone's mind that this was not accidental.

"On the morning of February 8 a new terror was sprung upon us. From the direction of Kamfersdam came the unmistakable screeching of a huge shell. The Boers, who had been noticed strengthening their works at that point, had mounted a 6-inch creusot gun, firing a 100-pounder shell.

"On the 9th the firing from this big gun began at daybreak and continued until late in the evening. The last shell fired that day did its deadly work only too well. Mr Labram, the chief engineer of De Beers Company and the clever maker of Long Cecil, while in his bedroom at the Grand Hotel dressing for dinner, was killed by a 100-pounder shell bursting in the room.

"Mr Labram was buried the evening after his tragic death, this time being chosen as it was unsafe to have a funeral by day. An enormous concourse of people had assembled to pay their last tribute of respect and honour to the man who had so materially helped in the defence of the town. No sooner had the clock struck eight, the hour of the funeral, than the alarm bugler's warning note rang out, followed by the whistling of a 100-pounder shell, steadily growing louder and louder as it sped on its baleful way. The mourners, nothing daunted, continued on their slow and sorrowful journey; shell after shell poured into the town that evening until near midnight, a respite coming with the birth of the following day, Sunday, which is strictly observed by the Boers as a day of peace and rest.

"Without doubt the Boers had a network of spies within the beleaguered town, who kept them fully cognisant of all that went on.

"I suppose we of the Town Guard had our humorous aspects ; but it must not be forgotten that to us was entrusted the work of watching a perimeter of ten miles, the handful of regulars being held in reserve to strengthen any threatened point. Newly raised, and in many cases absolutely without experience even in the Volunteers, we committed many errors, and the stock of stories of our humorous performances seemed illimitable.

"There was one of a mild man, lately joined, who had at least imbibed this principle, that for a sentry to leave his post was the gravest offence he could commit. It was a windy night, and he had not long been posted when a cry rang out, 'Sergeant of the guard,' which was soon repeated. Out rushed the gallant sergeant accompanied by his corporal, falling over the guard-tent guy ropes in his desperate hurry. We of the guard mean- while anxiously listened and groped for our rifles. The sergeant scrambled to his feet with all the haste he could, and in a hoarse whisper asked the sentry what was the matter. The 'budding Brodrick' nervously answered, 'I've lost me 'at.' I forbear from repeating the more forcible than polite comment which the sergeant made : no language could do the occasion justice. Our gallant sentry's hat had been blown off, and he thought a drum-head court-martial would be the inevitable result of walking a few yards from his beat to pick it up.

"I used to enjoy being on sentry-go at dawn. The lovely fresh air of the summer morning, the

first glimmer of light, then the gradual coming
of the delicate pinks, and finally (if there were any
clouds about) the glorious blaze of gold, blue, and
crimson which heralded the actual rising of the
sun—all combined to form a magnificent picture,
which in my case 'Brother Boer' never spoilt.
The twelve-to-two go and (in a minor degree) the
ten-to-twelve were to my untrained mind most
trying. However wide-awake when posted, in
about twenty minutes one felt that one would
give all one possessed to be allowed to sleep.
The pacing up and down seemed to have no
wakening effect, and I have sometimes found
myself reeling like a drunken man. In fact, as
time passed and no attacks were made, I came to
the conclusion that if death by shooting was to
be my fate it was much more likely to be at the
hands of my friends for sleeping on my post than
at the hands of my foes.

" It is extraordinary how callous one becomes if
not in a show oneself. We would watch artillery
duels between outlying forts just as unconcernedly
as, but with far greater gusto than, if they were
ordinary tennis matches ; and when on the clear
morning air the phit-phut of the mauser or the boom
of a gun was borne to us, we would turn over and

go to sleep again if satisfied that no projectiles were falling in our own neighbourhood.

" It takes a deal of shooting very often to hit anyone. One afternoon our mounted men went out beyond Bullfontein ; guns roared and rifles rattled for some hours, until I pictured the veldt strewn with dead, dying, and wounded. The actual casualties were — Boers, two wounded

Ambulance waggon.

(one mortally) ; British, one wounded (no bones broken).

" No account of Kimberley could even pretend to be complete which did not describe Long Cecil. Planned by the lamented Mr Labram, and constructed under the immediate supervision of Mr Goffe, both on the De Beers staff, it was made in an incredibly short time in the company's workshops. It was not until after Christmas that it was begun, and on January 19 it was actually tried. It was a breechloader, and fired a shell of 4·1 inches diameter, weighing about 29 lbs., the total length of the shell being $12\frac{3}{4}$ inches. Artillery officers consider its manufacture a marvel, when they call to mind the numerous departments that have to deal with the manufacture of a gun and its carriage in England, the numberless sighting and other

'Long Cecil.'

tests that it has to go through. It was served by the Diamond Fields Artillery, who made most excellent shooting, landing a shell on the Boer Long Tom the first day it fired, and, on the Boers' own showing, wounded five of the gun detachment : at any rate, Long Tom remained out of action for nearly twenty-four hours.

"Mention must be made of siege soup—the suggestion of Tim Tyson, then secretary of the

Kimberley Club, and as such known by now to nearly half the army. It was prepared at the De Beers Company's convict station. To look at, it was a thick grey concoction with lots of vegetables (a great boon to many who did not know where to get them), and it was guaranteed free from horse; but I 'ha'e ma doots.' It could be obtained in lieu of the horse ration, which many could not face. I hear you remark, 'But why? Surely the horse is a clean feeder?' Please remember that by the time you are driven to have recourse to horse, he is scraggy, under-fed, and rejected of the remount officer, and there is a general suspicion that he has been slaughtered to prevent death from other causes.

"No doubt, by the holding of Kimberley the De Beers Company, whatever it cost them, got the cheapest war insurance possible; but, on the other hand, the assistance afforded by them, and the time saved in dealing with one master mind like Rhodes, instead of numbers of individuals, must have been incalculable.

"De Beers held a large stock of food and fuel, horses, mules, and waggons; they possessed large engineering workshops, capable of producing a 4·1 inch gun in less than three weeks, and of manufacturing shells, not only for this gun, but also for the 2·5 inch R.M.L. guns, with which the Diamond Fields Artillery and the Royal Artillery were armed. Their three great searchlights for watching the 'floors' were invaluable at night, both

Horses on their last legs.

in scaring the enemy and in lightening the work of the sentries. They pumped all the water we needed, and by paying all their employés (deducting, of course, their military pay) they must have saved an immense deal of distress.

"Rhodes was splendid. He inspired confidence by the unconcerned way in which he rode about;

he supplied the military in an incredibly short time with what they wanted ; he planned relief works, such as road-making and avenue-planting, which Kimberley to-day is reaping the benefit of. He exposed himself in the most unselfish way while seeing that shelters were made for the inhabitants of Kenilworth, and that the women and children were received into the mines.

" Previous to the siege I was by no means an out-and-out admirer of Cecil Rhodes—in South Africa the majority of people seemed to find it possible to regard him only in one of two aspects, either as a demi-god or an arch-fiend—but he was magnificent during the siege, and one of the best men we had.   I think even General Kekewich, who is the pink of courtesy, will admit this.   That there was some slight friction one could readily believe.   It was inevitable with a military com-mander and a man of Rhodes' autocratic tempera-ment brought face to face in the same place, and that in the latter's own domain.   This will also be the more readily understood if you reflect for one moment that the military contribution was 500 men and a scanty supply of ammunition, and that of De Beers the bulk of the men, horses, food, and resources generally.

"The two Mayors, Mr Henderson and Mr Oliver, who held office during the siege, were excellent. The latter's mayoralty was during the more critical period, and he was absolutely fearless. Among our heroes we shall always number the dauntless Peakman (who succeeded to the command of the mounted corps on Colonel Scott-Turner's death); R. G. Scott, V.C., who was not deterred by the absence of an arm, which he lost in winning his cross eighteen years before, from rendering invaluable service with the mounted men; Major May, the cool commander of the Field Battery; Tom Rodgers of the Diamond Fields Horse, one of the born soldiers that times like these reveal, who deservedly got his D.S.O.; the gallant and cheery Bowen of the Kimberley Light Horse, who now seems little the worse for that bullet which shattered his jaw while charging the Boer redoubts in one of the sorties.

"Mention has been made of the searchlights, and this leads me to the subject of signalling. I well remember, the night of the battle of Modder River, the weird effect produced by the three great searchlight rays being all directed towards that place, waving slowly up and down endeavouring to call up Methuen. The next night, to our great joy, there was an answering flash, and shortly after regular communication was established, and press and private tele- grams could be sent. Later, this was supple- mented by helio communication by day to Enslin. The staff under Lieutenant De Putron and Lieu- tenant Wood- ward did magnifi- cent work as our telegraph de- partment for over two months,

and were specially complimented by the Director of Signalling.

"One of the most pro- minent features of Kim- berley during the siege was the 'conning tower' on the top of the hauling gear of the De Beers mine inclined shaft. A square erection was made

A 15-pounder shrapnel shell
after bursting.

supporting a roomy crow's nest. This commanded the whole country for miles around, and, as an officer was always on duty there, any move of the enemy could easily be detected. It was connected

by telephone with all the officers commanding
sections of the defence.

"I shall never forget the funeral of Scott-Turner
and the twenty-one who fell with him. The whole
town in mourning, the procession of representatives
from every camp and redoubt, and of the more
prominent members of the community, the seemingly endless stream of coffins, the lowering clouds
— for thunder showers were falling — the little
cemetery under the grim-looking *débris*-heap, the
volleys, the 'last post' sounded by the massed
buglers, and the homeward march full of fore-
bodings as to the future,—all combined to leave a
most Rembrandtian picture in the mind's eye.

"One word anent the Town Guard. They were
formed on the authority of the High Commissioner—not of the Colonial Government—and
considered themselves an Imperial force. At all
events, they had no connection with Sir Gordon
Sprigg's Colonial Defence Force, which arose nearly
eighteen months later. They provided their own
uniforms (with the exception of hats), blankets,
boots, and overcoats; they received only 10d. a
day ration money, instead of the Colonial allowance
of half a crown; so that, even to supply two meals
a day, some private contributions had to be made.

In the case of my redoubt we were not provided with any camp utensils, and even water was not laid on. Notwithstanding this, they have been refused the war gratuity promised to 'all troops.' Now, a great many were paid before this decision was arrived at ; many more joined some irregular force or other, and were paid in the corps they last served in ; so that I daresay not a thousand are left unpaid. Thus for a paltry £5000 a feeling of unjust treatment is left in the minds of a body of men who did their duty, and will come to the conclusion that, though they are called noble fellows in the hour of need, when the need has gone they are soon forgotten.

The conning tower.

"The story of the siege does not possess the dramatic incidents of that of Ladysmith or

Mafeking ; but by keeping the Boers in our neighbourhood, instead of their overrunning the Cape Colony, we were the humble, though perhaps involuntary, means of saving the Colony, and of thus rendering the Empire a tremendous service."

Much has been heard of the friction that was said to have occurred between the civilian portion of the garrison and the regulars. These reminiscences and impressions of one who as a civilian took part in the defence may throw some light on the exaggerated view that has been taken on this matter.

AFTER THE SIEGE

12 Burma mounted infantry

13   Mule transport crossing a drift

AFTER THE SIEGE

THE actual entry of the main body of the relief
column into the precincts of the Diamond City was
devoid of all dramatic or stirring incident.   One
or two civilians rode out to meet us on the outskirts
of the encircling line of redoubts, and a few ' Kaffir
boys' waved their hats and cheered as we passed
the first of the *débris* heaps outside Beaconsfield;
otherwise, for all that was apparent to us, it might
have been a deserted town that we had relieved.
General French and his staff, however, entered
the town itself and met with a very enthusiastic
welcome, being cheered again and again by the
delighted garrison.

The contrast to our entry into the capital of the
Free State was very marked ; but this was more or
less to be expected, as we reached the outskirts
of Kimberley in the growing dusk and bivouacked
outside the town, whereas our entry into Bloem-

fontein was in the full glare of day with a procession headed by our victorious Commander-in-chief.

Nevertheless, the impression left on one's mind would have been more appropriate had the circumstances been the reverse of what they actually were—had Bloemfontein been the relieved town and Kimberley the surrendered garrison.

I was told that many people did not even know that the town had been relieved until late in the evening. They had been disappointed by countless false reports for weeks, and the cry, "The relief column is coming!" fell on deaf ears, and was allowed to pass unheeded.

At five o'clock on the morning after the relief we were saddled up and awaiting orders, and it was not long before we were on the move. The day was spent in an engagement with the Boers who were occupying a position at Dronfield, covering the retreat of their guns and convoys. Thus we did not actually enter the town until two days after the relief. Our men never got more than a view of the outskirts of the city with its many chimneys, shaft-heads, and corrugated - iron roofs sparkling and flashing in the sun like so many brilliants.

To the casual observer the town itself at first

sight showed little real evidence of the fierceness of
the bombardment which it had gone through.
On approaching it by the Dutoitspan Road, the
first sign I
saw of the
work of the
Boer guns
was a huge
block of gra-
nite which
had been
bodily lifted
from the pavement and hurled
on to the roof of a house near
the Club.   Not many yards
farther on was St Cyprian's
Church, the roof and spire of
which had been slightly damaged.   Exactly opposite the
Club a shell from the Boer
Long Tom had plunged
through a photographer's shop,
making a huge hole in its exit
and bursting in the roadway;

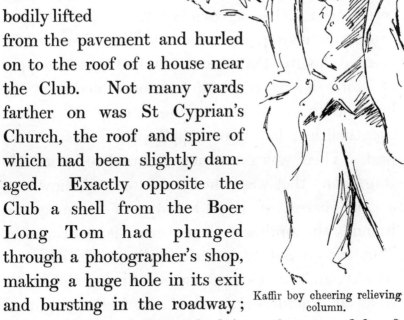

Kaffir boy cheering relieving
column.

fragments of it had crashed into the verandah of
the Club itself.   It was evident that the Boers had

made a determined but unsuccessful effort to wreck
the Club.

My object in going into Kimberley, however,
was not one of mere idle curiosity. Rather was
my errand in quest of supplies to replenish our
meagre mess stores, which were at a very low ebb.
I had to visit the Town Hall to obtain the necessary
permits from the Supply Committee. I thought
it only right to apologise for asking the citizens of
a town which had just withstood a siege of four
months to supply us with what they must have
sorely needed themselves; but I met with a most
courteous answer, and was told that there would
be no difficulty, that they really had a good supply
of stores in reserve. It had been necessary to
husband the available supplies, to guard against
eventualities; but now, happily, the necessity was
past. There was one thing I found it impossible
to get, and that was whisky. I secured, however,
a small barrel of Cape brandy—of some special
brand; the ordinary Cape brand is undrinkable.
This turned out to be an excellent substitute for
whisky, and not long afterwards, during the heavy
rains at Paardeberg, proved worth its weight in
gold.

Kimberley was never reduced to the straits that

Ladysmith was. At Ladysmith many of the commonest necessities of life ran out, and came to be looked upon as extravagant luxuries. Many ingenious plans were devised to circumvent their scarcity. For example, Tommy used to husband his matches by taking an old jacket and twisting it up into a tight roll; then he carefully applied a precious light to one end of this, and from the slowly smouldering pile innumerable pipes would be lit throughout the day. One match had done the work of several boxes. After securing my supplies, I could not resist the luxury of a visit to a well-appointed barber's. To realise what this meant to us—and I can assure you it is well worth the realisation—you would have to leave all vestiges of civilisation behind you for four months, and return with a beard of several days' growth and without razors and other necessary articles of toilet. This was how I entered Kimberley, and I was devoutly thankful that no 100-pounder shell had found its billet in the barber's pleasant shop. Kimberley at any rate had some compensations to make up for its lengthened siege. I then called on the Kimberley Club, of which we had, and most generously too, been made honorary members. I fear that during the four days we were

in Kimberley we ate them out of house and home,
and must have sorely tried the resources of their
genial caterer. This comfortable building had
come out of the bombardment unscathed, with the
exception of the slight damage to the verandah
previously mentioned, caused by a fragment of a
100-pounder shell. I had the good fortune to meet
there an officer of one of the Kimberley Corps, who
placed his house at the disposal of myself and two
brother officers. For the first time for many a
long day we enjoyed the comfort of a real shower-
bath, and emerged feeling more respectable and fit
to show ourselves in decent society.

A few spare moments for a ramble through the
town proved full of interest, as we came upon the
different results of the bombardment. Here was
a shop completely wrecked, another burnt to the
ground; there a hole in the wall large enough
to drive a coach and four through, corrugated-iron
roofs twisted and bent into every conceivable shape,
chimneys knocked down, and windows smashed.
Amid all those evidences of the recent shelling, the
surroundings appeared perfectly normal. People
quite unconcerned strolled about, doing their
shopping and other business, without so much as
glancing at the sights that interested us so greatly.

It was difficult to realise that these same people had just been through four months of a siege, with its bombardment, suspense, deprivation, and anxiety. We strolled into the theatre, the complete wreck of the inside of which clearly showed the disastrous effect of shrapnel when correctly burst. Twice had this building been a mark for the Boer guns.

As evidence of Mr Rhodes' practical forethought and help to the women and children, we came across an interesting notice, printed in large letters:—

"SUNDAY.—I RECOMMEND WOMEN AND CHILDREN WHO DESIRE COMPLETE SHELTER TO PROCEED TO KIMBERLEY AND DE BEERS SHAFTS. THEY WILL BE LOWERED AT ONCE IN THE MINES FROM EIGHT O'CLOCK THROUGHOUT THE NIGHT. LAMPS AND GUIDES WILL BE PROVIDED.

"C. J. RHODES."

This notice had been put up on the Sunday before (February 11). The Boer Long Tom had bombarded the town the whole of the day previous, and had continued doing so until close on midnight. As it was fully expected that it would begin again after twelve o'clock on Sunday night,—the Boers never broke the Sabbath,—thousands of women and children took advantage of the shelter offered by Mr Rhodes and proceeded to the mines. Others, who had the material and the means, constructed shelters of their own.   Some of these shelters might have been splinter-proof; but certainly none of them was bomb-proof.

The soil at Kimberley is only about 18 inches in depth, after which extremely hard rock is encountered; and thus dug-outs—the only safe shelters— were out of the question to all except those who

Splinter-proof shelter at Kenilworth.

happened to be living near a *débris* heap.   I saw one of these shelters made inside the courtyard of a house at Kenilworth, a suburb of Kimberley.

It was constructed with the open end facing Beaconsfield, in which direction no Boer guns were to be feared, and consisted of a solid wooden framework covered with corrugated iron, over which were heaped sandbags and earth.   The back was the weak point; it had only one thickness of sandbags. Seven feet in length, height, and depth, this shelter contained   a   light   spring-mattress   on   a   wooden

frame and an ordinary mattress ; and on the night
of Mr Labram's funeral, during which the town
was so heavily shelled, huddled up inside were
two ladies, two men, a baby, and a servant-maid.

Next day, Sunday, February 18, just one week
after we had concentrated at Ramdam—and what
an eventful week, both for ourselves and Kimberley !
—we were treated to one of the Diamond Fields
world - famed thunderstorms. These appalling
storms come on with alarming rapidity. First there
is the distant lightning ; then the faint rumbling of
the thunder, growing in volume every moment as
the gathering mass of black clouds is rapidly driven
before the approaching storm ; ere many minutes
have passed we feel the first heavy rain-drops ;
then, with a loud peal and a crash, the storm bursts
over us in all its fury.

It is difficult to realise in how short space of
time one can be practically left standing knee-deep
in water. Any little fall in the ground becomes
a rushing torrent, and the whole veldt around a
glistening sheet.

We had one consolation. The storm did not
come upon us in the middle of the night. Subsequent experience proved to us how thankful we
should have been for this.

When the worst of the storm had passed we
emerged from our various shelters, to find our few
remaining mess-stores floating about in the middle
of a newly-formed river, in which we had to
scramble for our dinner.

Boer manger at Olifant's laager.

Next morning we took our ponies to Olifant's
laager, to give them a well-earned day of grazing.
There was evidence here on all sides of the
hurried departure which the Boers had made.
Tents were even left standing; in one of them I
came across a case of very fine surgical instruments.
There was also ample proof of at any rate one well-
planted shell from the Kimberley garrison, a huge

gap having recently been made through one face
of the Boer redoubt; this the enemy had been no
doubt in the act of repairing when French's force
burst on their astonished gaze. The crowbars and
other implements with which they were digging
out huge rocks to patch up the gap were left lying

Olifant's laager.

where the Boers had dropped them in their hurry
to mount and be off.

I came across a Kimberley mining truck that
had evidently been used as a shelter. The occu-
pant of this must have been rudely disillusioned as
to its splinter-proof properties: in its side were
gaping wounds through which fragments of a shell
had torn their way.

Tuesday, February 20, was another welcome
day's rest for our ponies; but five o'clock next

morning saw us once more in the saddle and off
to Paardeberg.

We had a farewell dinner at the Kimberley Club
that evening. This dinner was marred by one
incident. At the end of the room a table had been
reserved for Lord Methuen and his staff, who were
to arrive by train from Modder River. Soon after

Kimberley mining truck used as shelter.

we had sat down, his commanding and handsome
figure, surrounded by several of his officers, was
seen. They walked into the room and took their
places amid a deathly silence. One felt the brutal-
ity of it. Surely Kimberley might have extended
some welcome to those who had so gallantly tried
to relieve it—who in attempting this had fought
four heavy engagements, three of these in one

week, suffering enormous loss, and had then the irksome task of facing Cronje's stronghold for over two months, without a sufficiently mobile force to outflank it and relieve Kimberley in the only way possible.

Surely she might have welcomed those who, by holding Cronje in front, not only prevented him from launching his forces into Cape Colony, but also enabled us to move round his flank—those who after having done this immense service, and after enduring many hardships, were forced to leave the actual relief of the town, with all its glamour and glory, to others. Of a truth,

" Fortuna obesse nulli contenta est semel."

In mentioning the impression received by me and others at the time, I may be doing Kimberley an injustice. If so, with a glad heart will I apologise.

From what I gathered during the few days I was at Kimberley, there seemed to be among the civilian portion of the garrison a certain amount of irritation, and certainly a good deal of nonsense was talked about 'red tape.' As a glaring instance of this, I heard quoted the first message transmitted by Lord Methuen to Kimberley, when signalling communication had presumably been established, which was to this effect: "Ascertain number on forefoot of horse issued to —— by the remount department Cape Town." The object of this message should have been obvious to the weakest intellect.

It is difficult to understand, in the first instance, why the Colonial Government were so tardy in recognising the important and perilous position of Kimberley in the event of a struggle between ourselves and the Boers. Owing to the indifference of, and want of encouragement from, the Colonial authorities, the Volunteer force in Kimberley had for all practical purposes, I am told, almost ceased to exist. The importance of the place can only be realised by studying its position on the map with reference to the two late Republics.

It will be seen that the heart of the town is only four miles from the Free State border. As a matter of fact, the Premier mine, one of the outlying points in the line of defence, the holding of which was rendered necessary to guard the water supply, is not more than a mile from the border. Bloemfontein in a direct line is only ninety miles, and not more than half that distance separates Kimberley from the late Transvaal border, while to the south-west was the strong rebel centre of Douglas.

It was not only owing to its importance as a
strategical point that the Boers were certain to
fling themselves upon Kimberley, but also on
account of the enormous riches of its mines and

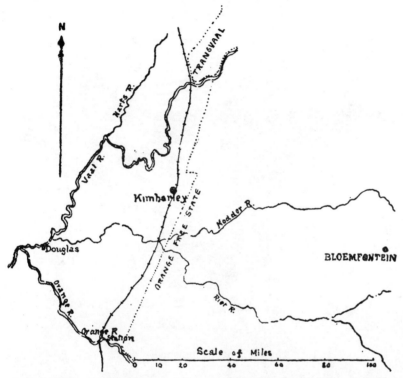

Sketch map showing relative positions of Kimberley and Bloemfontein.

the hatred which the two Republics had for the
late Cecil Rhodes, who was regarded as the king
of the diamond fields, making it a prize which they
could not for one instant be expected to lose sight
of. It was not to be wondered at, then, that the

Republics drew in their claws upon this priceless treasure.   The marvel rather was that they did not seriously attempt to take the town by storm.

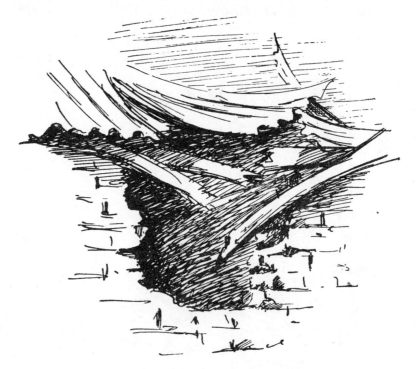

The effect of a 100-pounder shell.

SANNA'S POST

14   A Baralong fruitseller

15　Baralongs at Thabanchu

SANNA'S POST

On Tuesday, March 13,—what a combination for the superstitiously inclined !—we entered the capital of the Orange Free State, and bivouacked about three miles outside the town at Lawton's Farm. Two days later three companies of my regiment were sent to protect the waterworks, which are situated on the Modder River at Sanna's Post, about twenty-two miles east of Bloemfontein.

On Sunday the 18th was concentrated at Springfield, on the Ladybrand road, a few miles east of the capital, a small flying column, consisting of the 10th Hussars and Household Cavalry under Colonel Broadwood, one company 1st Mounted Infantry (the remainder being at the waterworks), Roberts' Horse, Rimington's Guides, Colonel Pilcher's 3rd Mounted Infantry, the Burmah Mounted Infantry under Colonel Alderson, and two batteries Horse Artillery (Q and U). This

105

column, the total strength of which was not more than 1300 men, was under the command of General French. Our destination was Thabanchu.

On the afternoon of that day we started on what proved to be a most eventful journey for all of us. Going out armed with a magnanimous proclamation of peace and goodwill, we returned with a veritable hornet's nest about our ears.

One cannot account for premonitions of coming danger; but certainly I began our march that day with a strange feeling that disaster would be the outcome of our mission. Our start was not what might be called auspicious. Hardly had we got under weigh when a terrific thunderstorm burst overhead. The rain came down in such torrents, and the driving hail with such force, that we were obliged to halt and turn our backs to it. I think this was the heaviest storm that I experienced in South Africa. We did no more than march to Boesman's Kop that night, which is about twelve or thirteen miles from Bloemfontein. One of the three companies of mounted infantry sent out to protect the waterworks was holding the Kop as a connecting post.

Next day the rain again dogged our footsteps. No sooner had we crossed the Modder at Sanna's

Post than down it came. Many wonderful ex-
pedients were resorted to by the troops to combat
the deluge, and weird-looking objects they appeared
with their waterproof sheets and blankets strapped
round them in every combination possible. We
bivouacked at Cameron's Farm that night, and next
day marched into Thabanchu without opposition.

A scene at Thabanchu.

Overshadowing the
small straggling village
is Thabanchu Moun-
tain, which, with its
rugged projecting
corner-piece, is a conspicuous landmark for miles
round. Thabanchu Mountain, I am told, means
the Black Mountain; but the most striking portion
of it is the huge block of white granite standing
out like a sentinel at its eastern extremity.

When passing the waterworks we were informed
by our mounted infantry, who were guarding it,
that the people in the farms about were friendly,

and anxious to give up their arms, the women even having begged them to come and take away the mausers and thus keep their husbands out of mischief. It was not long before the cunning and falsity of this demeanour was forcibly brought home to us. The following proclamation had just been issued by Lord Roberts, and part of our mission was to make it known throughout the district:—

V.  R.

"PROCLAMATION.

"To the Burghers of the Orange Free State.

"In continuation of the Proclamation which I issued when the British troops under my command entered the Orange Free State, in which I warned all burghers to desist from any further hostility, and undertook that those of them who might so desist, and were staying in their homes and quietly pursuing their ordinary occupations, would not be made to suffer in their persons or property on account of their having taken up arms in obedience to the order of their Government, I now make known to all burghers that I have been authorised by the Government of Her most gracious Majesty the Queen to offer the following terms to those of them who have been engaged in the present war :—

" All burghers who have not taken a prominent part in the policy which has led to the war between Her Majesty and the Orange Free State, or commanded any forces of the Republic, or commandeered or used violence to any British subjects, and who are willing to lay down their arms at once, and to bind themselves by an oath to abstain from further participation in the war, will be given passes to allow them to return to their homes, and will not be made prisoners of war, nor will their property be taken from them.

" ROBERTS,

" Field-Marshal Commanding-in-chief
" Her Majesty's Forces in South Africa.

" GOVERNMENT HOUSE, BLOEMFONTEIN,
    " 15th March 1900."

There is little doubt that many of the very burghers who, armed with these passes, had marketed their bread, butter, and eggs through

our camp, on the morning of the Koorn Spruit
ambuscade helped to swell the Boer ranks.

Thabanchu, from its associations, is a village of
more than passing interest. It nestles on the edge
of a small plateau with mountains rising abruptly
on the north and the impressive Thabanchu
Mountain towering above it on the east. Before
its annexation to the Orange Free State, it was

Thabanchu.

the capital of a small independent State belonging
to the Baralong tribe.

At that time also it was a large mission station.
The village, for the most part, consists of the
native location and the mission chapels. The
Baralongs are a particularly picturesque tribe ; the
dress for the men consisting as a rule of a blanket
thrown over their shoulders, more or less like a
Roman toga. Those of the most brilliant colouring
and loudest patterns were worn by all who wished
to be in the fashion. The effect of this was

marred by the head-dress and nether garments;
civilisation having here, as it seems ever prone to
do, stepped in to spoil man's
inborn taste for the picturesque.
I fear that before long the
blanket will have disappeared altogether, and its place be taken
by the ready-made half-guinea
suit.   A young Baralong, who
had no doubt been educated at
one of the Kaffir colleges, came
over to have a look at our camp.
If his ambition had been to ape
the English tourist, or 'Arry out
for a 'oliday, his get-up could not
have been better.   Compare this
man with the fine-looking Baralong fruit-seller, whose simple
but picturesque head-dress and

A young Baralong
at Thabanchu.

bare legs are thoroughly in keeping with the
blanket loosely thrown over his splendid shoulders.
This was the only man that I remember seeing
the *tout ensemble* of whose dress was unspoilt by
the European dealer's unsightly clothing.

I made sketches of many different types of these
people.   One of them was of a young Baralong

quite of the "masher" type. In place of the starched
linen collar reaching to the ears he had contrived
to convert his blanket, which was patterned with a
very loud and enormous cross check, into a long
kind of cape, a portion of which had been fashioned
into a turned-up collar; surmounting this, as might
have been expected, was a silly-looking head with
receding chin, covered by the smallest cap that
could possibly be induced to stay on. He was
talking to rather a fine-looking man riding a pony
with a staff pattern saddle and saddlebags; this
man's blanket had been supplemented by a pair of
Highlander's trews, brown leather gaiters, and a
straw hat.

By far the quaintest sight I remember seeing,
however, was in one of the Thabanchu stores, the
brilliancy of the interior of which, hung with
many bright-coloured blankets, handkerchiefs, and
chintzes, was in pleasing but violent contrast to the
hideous corrugated-iron exterior. Several Baralong
ladies were spending their monthly allowance in
dress; and to see these black women with their
good-natured faces chatting and laughing as each
in turn took up the different bright stuffs and in
front of a glass tried the effect, first in one light
and then another, of the varied colourings against

their dusky complexions, made me regret that I had neither pencil or brush at hand.

Many of the Baralongs have a very pronounced and unmistakable Hebraic cast of countenance. The manner in which they tried to drive a bargain gave me the impression that there was undoubtedly a strain of Jewish blood in their veins. One of our objects in going to Thabanchu was to collect supplies from this rich grain-producing district. It was amusing to watch Captain Foster and Captain Atcherley of the Army Service Corps endeavouring to strike a bar-

A Baralong.

gain with these people by the aid of an educated Baralong as an interpreter.

The Baralongs, like the Basutos, are great horse-breeders; and we secured some capital remounts in the Basuto ponies, which they freely brought in for sale at prices varying from £8 to £12. These ponies were not in the best condition when we got them; but they are wonderfully hardy animals, and where there is no grass, as in many parts of the Colony and the Transvaal, they will find food where the imported English or Irish horse would probably starve.

When ponies were brought in for sale there was always a third party, who professed to act as the disinterested go-between; his looks, however,

Notice over store at Thabanchu.

rather gave him away. A similar scene may be witnessed any day in Ireland; but in South Africa, instead of the whisky bottle being resorted to at the close of the deal, probably nothing more intoxicating than a bottle of ginger beer would be indulged in.

If one may judge from this placard, which was

put up over the store being used by the Army Service Corps as a supply office, the Baralongs must be a temperate people. I cannot quite recollect the interpretation of the whole notice; but spirits, I know, had no place in it.

Take notice!! Take notice!!

Tobacco   ——   ——

Lemonade, coffee, tea.

GINGER BEER.

The last, printed in bold lettering, was evidently the great attraction.

Our ten-days stay at Thabanchu was chiefly spent on outpost duty. On our arrival the natives informed us that a large force of Boers—about 6000, one man told me, which turned out to be fairly accurate—were trekking north with many waggons on the Wepener-Ladybrand road. This was apparently Grobelaar's and Olivier's forces retreating from Colesberg and Stormberg respectively with the idea of concentrating at Kroonstad, which town Steyn had declared his new capital.

The intention of the Boers at that time was no doubt to vacate the Orange Free State south of

Bloemfontein. Whether it was, emboldened by the subsequent disaster to our force at Sanna's Post and their success a few days previously at Brandfort — which village a small reconnoitring force of cavalry had entered and had been forced speedily to evacuate by an overwhelming force swooping down on them—or whether it was the knowledge of our enforced wait at Bloemfontein owing to the lack of remounts and supplies, the Boer forces that had so hurriedly trekked north doubled back, and again overran the southern portion of the Free State, threatening our lines of communication at every point.

The natural presumption seems to be that as soon as they recognised that we were, and would be for some time, unable to follow up their thoroughly disorganised forces beyond Bloemfontein, as we were dependent on our supplies being brought up by a single line of rails, and that their retreating force would have time to rally, the commandos that had hurriedly marched north to escape from what looked like an awkward position, and also with the object of helping to stem the tide of our forward advance, at once turned back to delay our advance by harassing our lines of communication in every possible way.

16   Buying ponies from Baralongs at Thabanchu

17   A patrol on the Ladybrand road

They seem for the first time to have awakened
to the knowledge of what a source of weakness to
us our lengthened lines of communication were,
and of what possibilities in that direction there
were for an enterprising and resourceful leader.
Such a man they found in De Wet.

The morning after our arrival at Thabanchu
Colonel Pilcher was sent in command of a small
column, consisting of one squadron 10th Hussars
and half the 3rd Mounted Infantry, to Leeuw
River, to destroy Newberry's flour-mills.   They
were situated on the Bloemfontein-Ladybrand
road, rather more than half way between Ladybrand and Thabanchu, which are, roughly, forty
miles apart.   The enemy having been reported by
Colonel Pilcher in strength near Ladybrand, next
morning Colonel Alderson took a squadron of
Cavalry, U Battery Horse Artillery, and the
remainder of the 3rd Mounted Infantry, some
distance along the Ladybrand road to cover Colonel
Pilcher's retirement in the event of his having been
attacked.   As Pilcher helioed to say that there
was no sign of the Boers intending to attack him,
the supporting column returned.

On the 24th he pushed on to Ladybrand itself,
and seized the landdrost and field cornet, being

received with apparent enthusiasm by the inhabitants. An officer of the 10th Hussars, who was told off to search the landdrost's house, in doing so became suspicious, owing to the palpable and persistent manner in which the landdrost's daughter, while pretending to be friendly, delayed him in his search by pointing out one thing and another of interest in the house and endeavouring to hold him in conversation. On leaving the house he found his suspicions only too well founded. No sooner had he put his foot outside the door than someone shouted " Hands up ! " Paying no heed, he jumped on to his pony—to find Colonel Pilcher's small escort leaving the town in desperate haste. The Boers were sweeping down on to the town in hundreds. The friendly shopkeeper of a minute before, dashing behind his counter, picked up his mauser lying in readiness there, and emptied its magazine at the men as they clattered past down the street. The local chemist, who was better suited to the concoction of pills than to the use of a rifle, in his hurry shot a passing Boer lady ; this regrettable incident, I believe, was the only serious casualty. The landdrost and field cornet were not allowed to escape, however. Seated in a Cape cart, while an officer, with a revolver pointed at the driver's head, rode alongside, they were driven out of the town at breakneck speed.

Colonel Pilcher retired to Leeuw River mills, and reached his destination in safety.

My company happened to be on picket that night at the Nek (on the Ladybrand road, about two miles east of Thabanchu). Between ten and eleven o'clock we heard the clatter of a horse galloping along the road towards the picket. This was an officer from Colonel Pilcher, bringing the news of the Ladybrand episode and of his retirement to Leeuw River. There seemed then every likelihood of the Boers following up this small column, who would have been in a very unenviable position had they done so.

It was not until nearly a week later—Friday, March 30—that the Boers made their descent on our small isolated force at Thabanchu. Meanwhile Colonel Pilcher had returned with his column. We were sorting our mails, which had arrived that morning, and I had just told the mess sergeant to get luncheon ready, when one of Colonel Broadwood's staff galloped over with an urgent message for us to saddle up, inspan, and await orders. Before many minutes had passed we were forming a screen to cover our retreating convoy, which, escorted by the 3rd Mounted Infantry under Colonel Pilcher, had been ordered to retire by the Bloemfontein road to beyond Israel's Poort.

My company was told off to hold the range of hills north of Israel's Poort,* about three miles to the rear, and was the extreme left of the semi-circle we formed to cover the retirement of the convoy, which was conducted without any untoward incident.

Late that evening we managed to get a few eggs and some bread from a native kraal—fortunately for us, as we had had nothing to eat since breakfast, and were destined to get nothing more until one o'clock the following afternoon. Our departure had been so sudden and unexpected that we were even without the usual biscuits.

At about ten that night we withdrew and continued our march to Sanna's Post, crossing the Modder at the waterworks about three in the morning. We bivouacked behind our outpost line about a mile west of the waterworks on the right of our convoy, which had preceded us and arrived two or three hours earlier. At four o'clock, thinking our troubles were over, we wrapped ourselves in our blankets, and, tired and hungry,

* *Poort* is Dutch for defile or gate.

soon fell into a sound sleep. At this very hour De Wet must have been stealthily creeping up the bed of the Koorn Spruit not more than a mile in rear of us.

Less than two hours later I was awakened by some rather hot rifle fire, which seemed to be coming from across the river on the Thabanchu road. A few minutes afterwards I saw what appeared to be some of our men between the kopjes east of the waterworks galloping in hot haste towards the drift. These turned out to be a patrol of the Rifle Company 1st Mounted Infantry (one of the two companies which had been guarding the waterworks). It had been sent out at day-break, and had not proceeded far before it ran into the Boers following hard on our footsteps of the night before. There had barely been time to realise what was happening when I saw the Boers gallop two guns round the foot of some kopjes across the Modder about two miles north-east of our bivouac, unlimber, and open fire on our camp. Shell after shell fell among the outspanned waggons immediately to the left of us.

Straggling, galloping horsemen were now to be seen streaming after their guns ; round and between these kopjes they came like a swarm of enraged

bees. We saddled our weary ponies, and formed
up a few hundred yards in rear of our bivouac,
the Boer gunners confining their attention for the
most part to the waggons. In next to no time

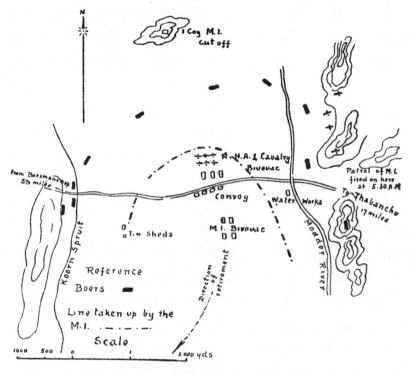

Diagram showing the ambush at Koorn Spruit.

the terrified native transport-drivers switched in
their teams and the leading waggons were wildly
tearing along the Bloemfontein road towards
Boesman's Kop.

The scene of excitement caused by struggling

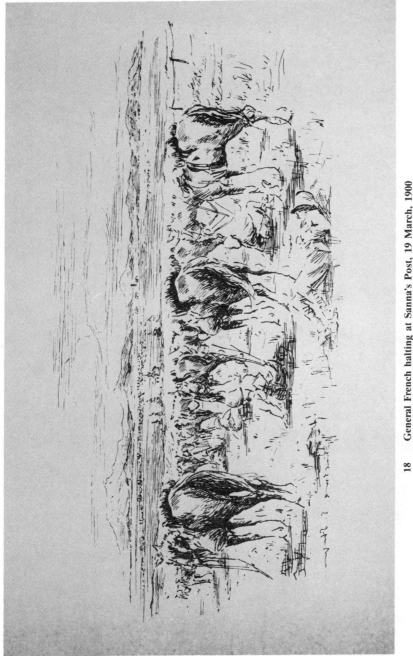

18   General French halting at Sanna's Post, 19 March, 1900

waggons enveloped in clouds of dust raised by the galloping and panic-stricken mules, urged on and frenzied by the hoarse yells of the drivers, the cracking of whips, and the hissing shells which, falling with a dull thud, threw up a cloud of earth as they ploughed into the ground, fortunately without bursting, now in front, now behind, in fact, everywhere save where the Boer gunners wished, soon passed. It was a relief to turn from this turmoil to our brigadier, Colonel Alderson, as, seated on his horse, he calmly took in the position and gave his orders, having apparently been told to form a baggage and a rear-guard with his mounted infantry. Our guns having moved off with the convoy, followed by the cavalry as escort, the Boer guns had it all their own way. Such a morning their gunners will not forget—a magnificent target in front of them never for one instant screened from view, and no answering shells to disturb their fire—how we longed for a gun that could not be outranged by theirs! Telling off Roberts' Horse under Colonel Dawson as escort to the convoy, the leading waggons of which by this time had disappeared into the Koorn Spruit drift, Colonel Alderson ordered my company to reinforce the remainder of the mounted infantry,

who had taken up a position to cover the retiring
waggons and guns.

Roberts' Horse moved off at a canter, and had
only for a second or two disappeared from view
after passing some tin buildings (the site of the un-
finished Sanna's Post railway station, from which
there was a slight fall in the ground to the Koorn
Spruit) about eight hundred yards in our rear, when
we were amazed to hear a terrific outburst of rifle
fire poured into them from the spruit. Such a
short distance intervened between us and the
Koorn Spruit that the company of Roberts' Horse
told off as a screen had not even had time to gallop
far enough ahead to warn the remainder following
close at their heels. We now fully realised what a
tight corner we were in, with Boers on three sides
of us, and no knowing yet whether they did not or
would not complete the circle. We were hemmed
in on an open plain, with no semblance of cover
other than the ant-heaps dotted about here and
there.

With this terrific fire, from which it seemed
impossible for any living being to escape, the Boer
ambuscade was unmasked. Roberts' Horse
wheeled about, and galloped out of the deadly
shower of lead. Our convoy had walked into a

trap ; but what had become of our guns and their escort ? As we anxiously looked towards the drift, riderless horses with loose swords dangling at their sides, and gun-team horses madly galloping through our ranks, soon told us that they, too, had not escaped the trap.

The batteries had been at the time moving on the right of the convoy. U Battery was leading, and, passing the waggons, which had come to a standstill owing to what appeared to be the usual block at a drift, halted as close to the spruit as possible, to await its opportunity of crossing. The leading company of Roberts' Horse, cantering along on the left of the convoy, arrived at this time abreast of the battery, and practically had reached the very edge of the donga when they found themselves confronted by a gleaming row of mausers. Their turning about to warn the companies following close on their heels was the signal for the Boers to reveal themselves and open fire. Under the deadly outburst of mauser fire that followed at point-blank range, men and horses of U Battery were mown down, and the guns, now helpless, were left at the mercy of the Boers. Q Battery, following behind, were enabled to wheel about, and, galloping some eight hundred yards back, with the loss of one gun in doing so, unlimbered and came into action.

Riderless horses, one or two carts, mule teams that had either been cut adrift or had broken their traces in their mad terror, and native drivers, were now seen wildly breaking away to the south, our only avenue of escape. Meanwhile Colonel Alderson had extended us in a wide semicircle stretching from the tin station-buildings on the left to the waterworks on the right, which flank was thrown back somewhat to prevent the Boers from working round in that direction. This had the effect of checking their advance, and prevented them from closing in on us. From whatever vantage-ground obtainable, they were content to keep up an incessant fire on us as we lay facing them in the open for over three hours. The least movement from any one of us instantly drew a heavy fire. Each one appeared to be marked down by a Boer rifleman. Lying here, we could see the tops of the waggons of the now captured convoy, so close and yet so hopelessly out of reach. Anxiously we glanced every few minutes towards the west, hoping for the welcome sight of a relief column appearing from Bloemfontein. Surely one must be on its way; but no! we looked in vain.

After some time my men began to run short of ammunition, and in going back to find the ammunition carriers I learnt what a mark was made of any slight distinction in dress. I had on a very light pair of breeches similar to those which we all took out to South Africa; they were very much lighter than those issued to the men (the only thing we could think of to assimilate them more to the men's was to soak them in strong tea or coffee). I only wore these as a rule when I thought we were going to have a peaceful day, an undeniable proof of how absolutely unexpected was our precipitate retirement from Thabanchu the previous day. The return journey with the ammunition carriers was even worse. The ant-heap selected in default of better cover was spotted by two or three persistent sharpshooters. One man's attention in particular I should willingly have dispensed with. He was armed with a Martini—this I knew by the much heavier thud and cloud of sand thrown up when his bullet struck the ground.

There were many narrow escapes that day. One of my men had just turned over on his side for a moment to get some cartridges out of his bandolier when a bullet buried itself in the very spot on which he had been lying. I will not weary you with more instances of this kind, though I could repeat such escapes by the score.

When the remnants of the guns (four of Q Battery and one of U), waggons, and led horses had been safely extricated and had got over the spruit at another crossing discovered about three miles south of the drift, Colonel Alderson ordered our retirement by successive lines. My company was the first to go, and took up a position farther back to cover the retirement of the remainder. The Boers, emboldened by our retirement, galloped up the opposite bank of the Modder parallel with our right flank, at the same time pressing on us from the west and the north. It was at this time Major Booth of the Northumberland Fusiliers gallantly gave his life away to save his men. He remained behind with his subaltern, Lieutenant Toppin of the same regiment, to keep up a fire to cover their retirement. Poor Booth fell riddled with bullets, and Toppin was captured. I saw the men pass me without officers, and feared some disaster had befallen.

We were followed for about two miles, the Boers galloping up and in many instances not even waiting to dismount, but firing off their ponies.

Eventually we formed up south of the Koorn Spruit, at about 11.30, crossing by the drift which the cavalry and guns had used earlier in the day.

As we rested here we saw the Boers shelling the kopje on which one of our companies, under Captain Radcliffe of the Devons, sent out on a reconnaissance from the waterworks at daybreak, had been cut off and surrounded. They were, happily, relieved, after a determined and stubborn resistance, having lost heavily in horses, but with few other casualties. We were ordered to continue our retirement to Boesman's Kop, which we reached soon after one o'clock, pretty well exhausted with hunger. We had had nothing to eat since break-fast the day before, with the exception of that which, as I previously mentioned, we got from the natives at Israel's Poort.

An unexpected surprise awaited us at Boesman's Kop. The first thing we saw was our mess sergeant with the mess Scotch cart, which we had never expected to see again, and a capital new team of six mules. Here he was calmly spreading out a luncheon for us as though nothing unusual had occurred. I believe this was the only cart that got away. How he managed to come out unscathed himself is perfectly marvellous. The native driver,

a very good boy, had been killed, our mess waiter
mortally wounded, and our mules shot. The team
with which he got out was a loose one which they
had caught galloping past them after their own had
been placed *hors de combat*. He told me that he
had had with him on his way out no fewer than
five native drivers, each one jumping off the cart
in turn and bolting when a shell dropped anywhere near. I think this was one of the finest
performances I heard of in a day that boasted of
many. I saw men with limp figures lying across
the front of their saddles galloping out that day ;
I saw men giving up their horses to wounded
comrades ; I saw others staying behind to help to
stop the flow of blood from a severed artery: but
for coolness and daring that eclipsed all this I
think we must look to those men who escaped
from out of the very gaping jaws of the ambush
itself—such men as Sergeant Clarke of the Nor-
folk Regiment, our mess sergeant.

One more surprise—we should hardly have felt
at home that day without surprises—awaited me.
As the evening was closing in and we were nearing
Bloemfontein, I could scarcely believe my eyes—
there was my groom with my favourite led pony
slowly riding on ahead !

When first we were shelled that morning I had told him to saddle up and be sure to keep with the waggons, thinking that they at any rate would get safely away.

I had pictured my groom a prisoner, if nothing worse had befallen him, and my little Irish mare in the hands of some burly Boer. This poor little beast plainly showed what she had been through that morning. She was perfectly terrified, and did not calm down until the welcome lights of Bloemfontein were well in sight.

My groom had been almost on the top of the drift when he saw the whole spruit lined with Boers. He was level with the leading company of Roberts' Horse when the fierce fusillade began. Hearing an officer shout out "Files about, gallop!" he had followed suit. His own pony had been almost immediately shot through the near fore and had come down; but she had quickly scrambled to her feet, and, throwing himself into the saddle, he had galloped on under a hail of lead. During the whole of this time he had clung on to my pony, which was carrying sixty sovereigns in my saddle-bags, that I had received the morning before from Bloemfontein to pay my men. Soon after this, he told me, he saw a doctor attending a wounded

man, and drew up to ask if he could be of any
help, but was told to go on, as he would only get
hit.   At that instant the doctor fell back dead,
shot through the heart.

He had managed to find a way across the Koorn
Spruit farther down, though he was nearly captured in doing so.

"But how was it the Boers managed to be
concealed so close behind you without it being
known?"   This is the question invariably asked
about the Koorn Spruit ambuscade. A natural
enough question too, and at first sight not an
easy one to explain. This was perhaps the most
daring and plucky piece of work of the Boers
throughout the whole campaign.   If the rein-
forcing column had arrived when expected, the
Boers in the spruit, even after they had captured
our convoy and guns, would have been in no
enviable position; and I can only surmise that
they were well aware of the time of departure
of General Colvile from Bloemfontein.

A disaster or a victory often hinges on a
trivial matter.   The full extent of this one, I
believe, was the direct outcome of the want of
initiative and the stupidity of a single patrol of
three men and an N.C.O.

It must be borne in mind that as soon as we had crossed the Modder that night we got behind the outposts of our mounted infantry, who had been guarding the waterworks for over a fortnight, and that behind them again at Boesman's Kop on our direct road to Bloemfontein there was another post held by our mounted infantry. Was not this fact alone enough to lull one into a feeling of security?

Moreover, it must be remembered, we only reached our bivouac in the blackness of the night and but two hours before dawn, no easy time to extend an outpost line. At daybreak, patrols were sent out to the east, north, and south. The usual patrol had gone to Boesman's Kop on the west at sunset, and should have reported themselves again in the early hours of the morning. This patrol, when returning, actually saw the Boers in Koorn Spruit, but made no attempt to give the alarm to their unsuspecting camp at the waterworks.

"Why, then, was not the convoy detained until another patrol had been sent towards Boesman's Kop when this one had not returned?" is the next question put. As our convoy was at the mercy of the Boer guns, I feel perfectly

certain that no one would have dreamt of keeping
them there, while an advanced guard was being
formed and sent off, on the thousand - to - one
chance of there being another party of Boers
behind us. I say another party, as those whom
we were retiring before could not possibly have
got there.

It is difficult to understand such intense stupidity as was displayed by the Boesman's Kop patrol;
but this we had at times to contend against. Reconnoitring, to be carried out to any good purpose,
requires men above the average intelligence, men
who have been specially trained and brought up
to it. No work in the whole war was more trying or called for greater individual initiative and
resourcefulness.

Our cavalry scouts, carrying their lives in their
hands each day, were, to my mind, the heroes of
the war—they were splendid.

The two subjects that to our critics are like
a red rag to a bull — which they one and all
have rushed at blindly — are scouting, or rather
the want of scouting, and the want of taking
cover. How many of them have actually seen
our scouts at work or our men taking advantage
of cover when within the effective zone of fire?

I don't think many; yet they pose as authorities on this subject.

I will give one instance of the length to which the criticism was carried. A day or two after Sanna's Post, Captain Atcherley (I think it was) was looking over my sketch-book, and we were remarking on the bareness of the veldt and the utter lack of cover between the waterworks and the Koorn Spruit, when one of the most influential and best known—I might say quite the most influential—of the war correspondents broke in on our conversation with this remark: "No cover? What nonsense! In half an hour I would dig up enough cover with my penknife."

To those who know that part of the country, the absurdity of this remark will be apparent. Of course, I do not take this too literally; but I would give this correspondent the most improved entrenching tool in place of his penknife and let him try under the same conditions to throw up cover for himself, and would wager that within two minutes he would gladly hand that spade to someone else and take his chance by lying as still as he could and using his rifle with the least movement possible.

The bare fact of raising a rifle to one's shoulder

was sufficient to attract the fire of two or three Boer marksmen.

"For all right judgment of any man or thing it is useful, nay, essential, to see his good qualities before pronouncing on his bad."—CARLYLE.

THE CROSSING OF THE VAAL

THE CROSSING OF THE VAAL

AFTER an irksome delay of a week at Kroonstad, we began our northward advance to the Vaal.

Kroonstad, we were told, was the favourite watering-place of Johannesburg. With such a reputation, a more disappointing place I cannot imagine. From outside, with the roofs of the houses and the church just showing above the tree-tops, it looked quite an inviting spot. Its appearance, however, was deceptive. On entering the town we found nothing but a few dirty, dusty streets lined with badly-built shanties. It certainly was not looking its best at this time. Many of the stores were roughly barricaded and rendered unsightly with ugly hoardings; and those which were open appeared to be denuded of almost everything, commandeered by the various commandos passing through.

There was one decidedly pretty spot; and that

was the beautiful broad stretch of the Valsch River skirting the south side of the town, formed by a well constructed dam lower down the river. Studded along its finely-wooded banks were a few pretty, red-tiled, English-looking villas, at one of which the headquarters staff had taken up their abode.

Everything pointed to the Free Staters giving in. The landdrost's office was thronged each day with burghers coming in to give up their arms and take the oath of allegiance under the terms of Lord Roberts' Proclamation of March 15. These burghers told us that all the Free Staters were heartily sick of the war and would not cross the Vaal: once we got there, they would give in. They expressed themselves as very bitter against the Transvaalers, who, they stated, had done all the damage they could, and when we appeared were the first to run. Of course, all this had to be accepted with reserve; but we were, I think, justified in our belief that a strong resistance at the Vaal, Johannesburg, and then Pretoria, would see the end of the war.

That there was some cause for bitterness at the destruction wrought throughout the Free State we realised on entering the Transvaal. The contrast between the two countries was most marked. The Free State, with the wholesale wrecking of its station buildings, the complete demolition of its bridges and culverts, the railway torn up everywhere and telegraph wires down, presented a pitiable appearance; whereas in the

Destruction of the Valsch River railway bridge.

Transvaal there was nothing of this—neither the bridges nor the railway had been damaged.

Leaving Kroonstad on Sunday, May 20, we marched north to Boschkoppies, which are not more than twenty miles distant, in two easy stages. The first night we bivouacked at Doorn Spruit, a tributary of the Valsch River. In the distance we could see the ugly mountains that stood guard over the banks of the Rhenoster River. These,

we were informed, were strongly held as a bar to
our farther advance.

Boschkoppies were reached about three on the
afternoon of the 21st. Hearing that the drift over
the river, about six miles farther on, had been
occupied unopposed by some of our cavalry in the
morning, Colonel Alderson pushed on in support
with two companies of the 1st Mounted Infantry
and some guns. This drift is immediately below
the junction of the Honing Spruit with the
Rhenoster River, and is commanded by a range of
high kopjes on the right bank. Had the Boers
held it, as we fully expected when we marched off
that morning, we should have had a difficult task
in dislodging them.

Pushing our outposts beyond the Honing Spruit
that night, we crossed the drift next morning.
Not only had we encountered no opposition, but
also no fewer than between thirty and forty
Free Staters surrendered to us here. They all
professed themselves as highly delighted at giving up their mausers, and as sick of fighting.
This, I am certain, was a genuine expression of
the feelings of the majority of them. Many,
we discovered, were old friends of ours! They
belonged to De Wet's commando, and had been

in the Koorn Spruit ambuscade. They were rather interested to hear that we were the men they had hoped to capture that day.

One of my men, belonging to the Manchester Regiment, they remembered well: he was actually with the waggons when these were captured, and it was only by using the butt-end of his rifle that he got away from a couple of Boers who were attempting to make him a prisoner. I heard them laughing and joking to him about this episode. One of those two burghers, they said, would carry the mark of that rifle to his dying day.

We bivouacked that night about four miles north of the drift, near the foot of the hills, with a wide, open plain stretched out before us. General French's cavalry division were encamped about four or five miles farther on. We were not destined to have much rest. At three the next morning, leaving our transport behind, we silently marched on in the wake of the cavalry, following the course of the Essenbosch Spruit. No fires were permitted, and no smoking was allowed. Not a sound, save the occasional clanking of a bit or the muffled "Hold up!" to a stumbling pony, disturbed the stillness of the night.

Soon we passed through the recently vacated

camping-ground of the cavalry. Their transport waggons and mules, dimly outlined, every now and then loomed up, spectral, behind the black veil enshrouding everything.

Then the first glimmer of light in the east heralded the dawn. Over the top of the cold grey mists hugging the glistening veldt, we could see on our right the Rhenoster kopjes faintly outlined against the lightening sky. This was the position athwart the railway which was reported to be strongly held. Our object was to get behind the Boers and place ourselves astride their line of retreat; while General Ian Hamilton's column were to operate on the right, and the Headquarters Division in front. This meant a march of at least twenty-five miles before we could be in a position to carry out our share of the scheme.

On reaching Essenbosch, about fifteen miles from our bivouac of the day before, we halted, and there heard that the Boers had already vacated their entrenchments and hurriedly fled north.

When we started from Kroonstad, a strong opposition to our advance was expected at the Rhenoster River. Our enforced wait there of seven days had offered the Boers every facility to concentrate their disorganised troops; and the

Stratford & Shee

20   Our water supply at Kroonstad

21   Led ponies

well-defined chain of kopjes guarding the bed of
the river gave them a natural line of fortifications,
and paved the way for a stubborn resistance.

Before marching off, General Hutton, in address-
ing our brigade, said that we were now entering
upon perhaps the most momentous week of the
war. With this foreboding we left Kroonstad.
As soon as we found that the Boer position at
the Rhenoster River had been abandoned we concluded that the Vaal was being made impregnable.
Subsequent events will show how far this surmise
was correct.

Early on the morning of Thursday, May 24,
we marched off from Essenbosch in the keen hope
of setting foot on Transvaal soil that night. The
news that this had been safely accomplished, we
knew, would be a welcome birthday greeting to
our Queen. Over the rolling grass downs we
swept along, gazing north with expectant eyes.
At length, through the dancing heat-haze a long
line of distant blue mountains could be faintly dis-
cerned. This was our first view of the Transvaal.
Twisting and bending at the foot of these mountains, our maps showed us, was the broad Vaal.

As we drew nearer, a more forbidding country
could not be imagined. There was a seemingly

endless chain of high rugged mountains forming
a natural fortress to guard the boundary. Like a
decoy bird in front was the peaceful-looking little
town of Parys, nestling in a bed of trees, with its
church towering high above the surrounding house-
tops, as in some pretty English village. And now
we caught our first glimpse of the silvery Vaal
bending round the foot of a kopje north of the
town.

Why did not those mountains reverberate and
echo with crash of shell and roar of rifle fire?
Surely, with such a stronghold, the Boers would
never let us put foot across the river without
resistance? Could it be the ominous calm before
a storm?

Our cavalry had now reached and were moving
along the very banks of the Vaal itself beyond the
village, and not a shot had been fired.

At last a sign of life appeared on the far
side of the river. What were those scattered
horsemen, mere specks in the distance, cantering
along the crest of the kopje overhanging the
Vaal, and that formed body below?

Every nerve was strained; every eye was fixed
on them. There could be no mistake. Undoubtedly they were our own men.

Our cavalry had crossed the river and set foot in the Transvaal without a shot having been fired. For the third time within a fortnight—at Kroonstad, Rhenoster River, and now here—we had gained our objective without the heavy fighting we expected. We were reaping to the full the fruits of Kimberley, Paardeberg, Poplar Grove, Drie-fontein, and the Zand River. The Boers had been unable to recover from their demoralised retreat.

One cavalry brigade crossed over by the drift at Parys, which was impassable for guns or waggons, and moved up-stream along the north bank, parallel with the main body on the south bank. We followed the latter with the transport and supply column. The road running along the bank of the river is hemmed in by rugged kopjes covered with loose boulders and shrub. One could not help thinking how small a force of Boers would have sufficed to hold the drift and make this road im-passable to us. Losing touch with French at this time was one of the greatest blunders of the Boer leaders. General French had outwitted them, and gained the crossing of the Vaal at a point where they least expected him.

The remainder of the cavalry division, with their guns, crossed the river at Viljoen's Drift—where

the frontispiece sketch to this chapter was made—
about nine miles north of Parys.   General Hutton,
with all the transport, remained on the south bank.
We had covered about thirty miles that day ; and
it was late before our transport arrived.

Next morning we crossed the Vaal, happy in the
thought of at last standing on Transvaal soil, and
seemingly within measurable distance of the end
of the war.   Relieving the cavalry outposts, who
pushed on up the river to Lindeque, we followed
as a rear-guard.   No time was lost in getting clear
of this mountainous district.   Advanced parties of
Boers were even now hovering on our left flank ;
but these were easily driven off by the cavalry,
securing the passage of the Lindeque drift for our
transport, who, escorted by Colonel Pilcher's
Mounted Infantry, kept along the south bank and
crossed at that place.

KLIPRIVERSBERG

KLIPRIVERSBERG

Having secured a firm footing in the Transvaal, we were all impatient to push on. Speculation was rife as to what opposition we should meet with at Johannesburg and Pretoria, which places, we expected, were to witness the final struggles of the war.

Leaving Lindeque on May 26, we crossed the Riet Spruit, and late that afternoon met with some slight opposition, which kept us out until well into the evening. There was great difficulty, afterwards, in finding our camp. A mounted force such as ours, with guns, transport, and supply column, occupies a large area of ground ; and in the dark we wandered about for a considerable time before getting any tidings of our bivouac. I fail to see why each brigade should not have a distinguishing lamp. There was often the same difficulty with our transport and led ponies when they came in

after dark.   I have even known cases where men
with led ponies, although wandering about within
a short distance of their camp, have failed to find it,
and not turned up until the morning.   As we were
dependent on them for our blankets and kit, this
was no trifling matter.   Our bivouac that night

A Royal Canadian.

was near the banks of the Riet Spruit, about eight
miles west of Vereeniging.

Next morning we occupied some high kopjes, four
or five miles south, overlooking that town, and then,
turning back north, followed in the wake of the
cavalry, and bivouacked at about six in the evening
at Doornkuil.

We had barely off-saddled when a message came
from General French ordering a regiment of
mounted infantry to be pushed forward immedi-

ately.   My battalion was told off for this, and after
our dinners we started off without delay.   It was a
very dark night, and in consequence our going was
slow, and we did not reach our destination until
about twelve o'clock.   We then relieved the
majority of the outposts thrown out by the cavalry,
who late in the afternoon had seized the formidable
Gatsrand range of mountains, which, lying directly
across our line of advance and running for many
miles due east and west, would have formed a
strong barrier to our northern advance had the
Boers been left to hold them.   In accomplishing
this, General French had only just forestalled a
large force of Boers who, coming post-haste from
the Potchefstroom district, having failed in their
primary object of preventing our crossing the Vaal,
turned their attention to blocking our farther
progress at this important point, but found themselves again outmanœuvred by his intrepid dash
and nerve, and driven off from the slight footing
they had obtained on the Gatsrand.

From this lofty eminence we obtained a magnificent view of the country stretching away to the
north, broken first by the Klipriversberg and then
by the distant blue Witwatersrand range.   We
were now but fifteen miles from Johannesburg, the

old coaching-road to which could plainly be traced as it wended its way first over the Klip River, across the plain beyond, and then over the Klip-riversberg hills.

I shall never forget the bitter cold of that early morning on the Gatsrand. The raw wind rushing up its steep slopes went through us like a knife. It was but a foretaste of what we were to experience that night.

We watched the cavalry, supported by General Hutton with the remainder of the Mounted Infantry, pushing on over the Klip River to the open plain beyond. When the rear of this column was clear of the Gatsrand, we were relieved by the baggage guard, and followed on to join Colonel Alderson, who had crossed over the Olifants-vlei bridge with the Canadians, and in conjunction with the cavalry, under a heavy fire, had seized the first low spur of the Klipriversberg.

As we crossed the river General French was directing operations from a small kopje on the right of the bridge. I am afraid the sketch opposite does not give any idea of the heavy shelling that the cavalry were subjected to from long-range guns. General French is the centre figure. In successive lines, well extended, with their left

resting on Olifantsvlei, the cavalry were circling
round the ridge, now securely held by Colonel
Alderson.   The Boers opened a well-directed shell
fire as our troops swept over the plain.   We,
keeping to the right of the Johannesburg road,
opened out, and rode directly to the ridge already
held by the Canadians.

The cavalry mono-
polised most of the
Boer fire.   It was only
when our ammunition

General French directing the engagement at Klipriversberg.

carts followed us that a few well-aimed shells,
whistling over our heads, plunged into the ground
a few yards from them—they being mistaken for
guns, I imagine, by the Boer gunners.   These carts
were invariably a sure draw for the enemy's fire, and
we always preferred them to keep a safe distance in
rear of us.   After having reinforced the Canadians,
we spent the remainder of the morning watching
the Boers on a ridge facing us about a mile in front.

While the cavalry, now out of sight, were pushing on, there was a lull in the fire, and during this time, no doubt, every available Boer gun was being silently got into position, awaiting an opportunity to unmask on them. To us everything appeared to be proceeding successfully, and at about three in the afternoon the transport crossed the Klip River, and followed in the track of the cavalry. But if the latter were succeeding in their purpose, why were the Boers holding the ridge in front of us so amazingly confident? There they coolly sat dangling their legs over the crest, only disappearing behind their scantzes when our pom-pom fired on them. Their flippant behaviour did not show the least anxiety as to their position. In reality, both of us were performing identically the same *rôle ;* but, whereas we were holding the enemy so as to permit of a successful turning movement, we took it that they were a portion of a rear-guard whose object was to delay any advance on our part and enable them to get their heavy guns away. This idea, however, could not be reconciled with their present demeanour.

With our horses sheltered close under the steep slope of the ridge, half of them being off-saddled, most of us were lazily lying about waiting for

C1   A veldt fire

C2   The ox wagon

C3   Wire cutters to the front

C4   Tapping telegraph wires

C5   Shoeing in the veldt

C6   Under shelter of a kopje

C7   The road out of a drift

C8   War balloon on the march

C9   Transport formed up

C10   A Cape cart from Cronje's laager

C11   The rush for Kimberley

C12   After a storm at Kimberley

C13   Guard mounting, Bloemfontein

C14   Examining a boer's pass

C15   Some types of Free State farmers

C16   Transport crossing a swollen drift

C17   Watering horses

C18   Transport, Lumsden's horse

C19   Free State burghers surrendering at Kroonstad

C20   Our brigadier's buck-wagon

C21   Tongas crossing a drift

C22　The contents of a captured boer wagon

C23　A midday rest

C24   Mounted infantry stretcher bearers

C25   General French's first view of the Transvaal

C26   Saddling up at Viljoen's Drift

C27   Shell falling among Tongas

C28　First mounted infantry at Klipriversberg, May 29, 1900

C29　Mounted infantry coming down the Witwatersrand

C30   Evening at Welgelegen

C31   Nearing Pretoria

the next move. This suddenly came from a quite unexpected quarter.

I had just taken out my note-book, and was pencilling in a little sketch of the tongas halted on our left, when suddenly, unheralded by the usual warning crescendo hissing screech, with a whizzing crash a shell from one of the high-velocity

A tonga.

Krupp guns fell within a few feet of the group I had just left, bursting into fragments on impact with the hard rock. One piece hit the horse I was on the point of sketching. Right under the kopje as we were, the sound of its approach was masked, and came upon us quite as a surprise. This gun must have opened fire at a very long range, and it was a revelation to us how shell fire can search the reverse slope of a steep hill. Our pom-pom was immediately above us; and without doubt it was this little gun, which had been making itself objectionable to them, that the Boers were endeavouring to silence. The correct range must have been estimated to within a few yards. Obviously this was no place for our ponies, which I moved farther to our left. Our tongas, which were on the main Johannesburg road, in order to follow suit were obliged to turn about and retire some hundred yards, owing to there being a deep ditch on either side of the road. In doing this they came under a severe shelling. Whether they were seen and mistaken for our pom-pom retiring, I cannot say; but three shells from the Boer Long Tom came shrieking after them in quick succession.

The Indian tonga wallas stood the first two shells gallantly; but the sound of the third approaching completely unnerved them. Throwing themselves down on their knees, they offered up a fervent prayer to Buddha.

It was a miraculous escape. The shell fell on to the road immediately behind the tongas, but did not touch a soul. This was the last attempt the Boers made that afternoon to silence our pom-pom.

There was another lull—this time before a storm

in earnest, the full brunt of which was met by
the cavalry. A cloud of dust heralded the first
tidings of its coming. Following this were seen
the transport waggons and led ponies hastily
beating a retreat towards Olifantsvlei. Something
was wrong; but what had happened?

We were not long left in doubt. A disconcert-
ing picture now presented itself as shell after shell
fell among the waggons. In appearance it was an
exact replica of our convoy racing for the Koorn
Spruit drift. Close on their heels came the rear-
most squadrons of the cavalry, followed by the
remainder with their guns hidden at times by the
clouds of earth and sand thrown up by the plunging shells from the Boer long-rangers. Every ridge
belched forth its missiles, from the spiteful little
pom-pom one-pounders to the heavy projectiles of
the high-velocity Krupp guns. The Boers must
have unmasked at least a dozen guns from the
centre and the right of their position, which was
shown to extend to the ridges west of Olifantsvlei. It was preparatory to this outburst that
we on the right had been comparatively left
in peace. This also accounted for the assured
confidence of the Boers on the ridge facing us.
We had failed to turn their position, which

appeared to be far more extended than was at first surmised.

After the retirement of the cavalry General Hutton was left to hold the line of ridges which we were occupying, while General French recrossed the Klip River and bivouacked on the far side.

Throwing out a line of outposts, we remained in position until relieved by the cavalry between eleven and twelve o'clock. This was a most trying night. As the sun set the temperature rapidly fell below freezing point, and the grass under our feet became crisp and white with the heavy frost. Hungry and tired after a second long day, with no rest the night before, merely wrapped up in their overcoats, the men flung themselves down and slept at their horses' heads. It seems almost incredible, looking back on it now, but I know that personally I woke up to find that I had fallen asleep in that frost-coated veldt without any addition to my clothing except a cardigan waistcoat. My cloak I had thrown across my little Irish mare's back, and I have no doubt many others did the same.

Reaching our waggons, which were outspanned at Olifantsvlei, about one in the morning, and welcomed by a roaring fire, we sat down to our

belated dinner. Our orders were to remain ready
saddled-up, and we were early astir to relieve
the cavalry outposts. There was a dense mist
overhanging the veldt, and we woke to find the
water in our buckets covered with thick ice.

After a hasty breakfast, under cover of the mist

Transport drivers.

we once more advanced through the smouldering
veldt, set alight by the shelling of the day before,
to take up our position on the ridge we had
occupied the previous night. This was to be held
by us as a pivot for the turning movement of
the cavalry, which this time was to be on a much
more extended scale. When the mist lifted, we,
now on the extreme left of the holding line,

found ourselves in a particularly uncomfortable position—at the end of a wedge, as it were, shoved in between the re-entrant angle of the

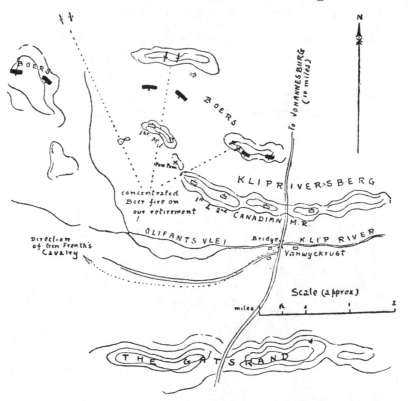

Plan of position held by Colonel Alderson.

Boer position. The kopje we were holding could be raked by shell fire from commanding heights on right, left, and centre. We watched the cavalry moving off, soon to be followed by another long column pouring down the steep

Gatsrand Pass in a whirl of dust. This was Ian Hamilton.

From the Boers not shelling us on this exposed position more than they did, I conjecture that they were too much occupied with the dreaded turning movement on their right flank to pay much attention to us. Until shortly before our retirement they had only brought two pom-poms into action against us from the kopje on our right. Fortunately, the range was rather over-estimated. The far slopes of our ridge had been set alight, and our skirmishers had to keep falling back before the irregular wave of burning grass steadily sweeping on towards them. The Boers meanwhile crept up under cover of the blinding smoke, and at one time it looked as though they intended rushing our position. The ridge across the stream on our left, we could see, was strongly held. To our amazement, we saw our troops working their way up the reverse slope—at first a few scattered little figures creeping from rock to rock, met by the desultory click-clock of the mauser, which soon swelled to a continuous roar as the surging lines of khaki pressed on up the bullet-swept slope. These were the Gordons pressing home General Ian Hamilton's attack. At the same moment Colonel

Alderson began to extricate us from our somewhat precarious position, this being the signal for the Boers to unmask their guns, in much the same manner as they had done the afternoon before on the cavalry. Bringing two guns into action from the kopje on our right, they subjected us to a galling cross-fire. As each successive line retired from one position through the next, all the available Boer guns were turned on to it. Personally I retired my company, which was the last to leave, a section at a time, the men extended to between thirty and forty paces. After the first two sections had left, seeing that the Boer gunners on our right had the exact range of the ground over which they had retired, and as these guns enfiladed us and were the most to be feared, I ordered the next section to retire by a different line. I had just pointed out the direction I wished them to take, and given the order to mount, when, as if the enemy were divining my thoughts, a shell plunged into the ground not ten yards off (we were holding a small isolated kopje at the time) on the identical line I had selected for the left of my retirement to rest. The ground was torn up in every direction by the falling shells as, extending from behind our cover, we debouched into the open. It was a marvel to see men, almost completely hidden in clouds of dust from falling projectiles, emerging unharmed. Shell after shell burst over each extended line. The Boers' marksmanship was excellent. Had we not had room to open out it must have wrought tremendous havoc. Their segmental and shrapnel shells were evidently aimed too high: at any rate, they did no damage.

Royal Canadians and 1st Mounted Infantry forming up. Klipriversberg.

One burst directly overhead, and I saw the segments harmlessly striking the ground, without even embedding themselves.

We recrossed the Klip River by Olifantsvlei bridge, and formed up on the slopes of the Gatsrand. Men and horses were now thoroughly done up. The former simply fell asleep from sheer exhaustion.

Our ponies had been saddled up for practically

sixty hours. Only twice during that time had we been able to ease them of their saddles, and then for not more than two hours at a time. We had done three days' and two nights' hard work with at the most six hours' regular sleep.

The whole of the Klipriversberg ridge, which we had just vacated, and the grassy plain in front, was now in flames, set alight by the continuous heavy shelling. When all were safely across the river we followed in the wake of the cavalry, and bivouacked at Doornkop, memorable as the scene of the surrender of Dr Jameson and his men. Evidences of the fight were discernible in the scantzes built by the burghers, which were still standing.

General French's turning movement had been successful, and the Boers were in full retreat. Pushing on north next morning, we crossed the Potchefstroom-Johannesburg railway between the Roodepoort and Florida mines. A continuous line of shaft heads and tall chimneys stretching some ten miles east marked the track of the railway to Johannesburg.

We now came to the rocky heights of the Witwatersrand range. While picking our way down the farther side we espied a Boer convoy in

front of us hastening some two miles off along the
Pretoria road. Instantly giving chase, and driving
in their rear-guard, we captured a number of
waggons and prisoners. The Boers were in rather
a miserable plight. Throwing down their arms,

Florida Mines.

they came running in, holding their hands high
above their heads, so that there should be no mis-
taking what they meant.

One more stage of our advance to Pretoria had
been successfully concluded.

22   Captured boer wagons

23   A Transvaal burgher

LIFE ON COMMANDO

LIFE ON COMMANDO

I AM indebted for the information and the anecdotes to be set forth in this chapter to one who was a burgher of the Transvaal Republic, and wishes to remain anonymous. He says that various writers have attempted to pourtray the life of the Boer on commando, but that in many cases the information given has been meagre, vague, and often fanciful. As the subject has become of unusual interest through the men who gave us so much trouble during the late war having become our fellow-subjects, I will transcribe my informant's account of the doings and life of the Boers on commando.

The whole of the land covered by the late Transvaal Republic and the Orange Free State was divided up into districts corresponding to our counties. A district might, for fiscal purposes, be divided into wards or areas, each under a field cornet appointed by the Government, the whole

under a commandant elected for a term of three
years by the burghers of that district. The term
'commando' was given to a body of men drawn
from the area under the fiscal supervision of a
field cornet. As regards the formation of a
commando, the field cornet was the man responsible for its mobilisation. On his shoulders most
of the work fell, and his powers were practically
despotic. He had a list of all the burghers in his
ward. A commandier briif[1]—that is to say, a
mobilisation order—was issued by him to all the
burghers stating that, owing to a state of war
between the Transvaal or the Orange Free State,
as the case might be, and England (to instance the
last case), their presence was ordered at the market
square of the village or dorp,[2] should the field
cornetcy include the village, on such and such a
day. In the case of an outside district the commandier briif would order the burghers to assemble
at the field cornet's farm.

The order would inform them that they were to
bring with them an equipment, consisting of a horse,
saddle and bridle, a rifle and bandolier with fifty
rounds of ammunition, and provisions. Eight days'

[1] Letter.

[2] Village (white man's); a native village is kraal.

provisions were always demanded ; but as a matter
of fact the commando lived at the public expense as
soon as they were near enough to a commissariat
base to draw supplies.   The supply of provisions
ordered to be brought would not, however, cause
much trouble or be a heavy burden to carry, as this
mainly consisted of biltong and biscuits.   Biltong

Boer cart.

is meat (a portion of a buck, as a rule) cut up into
strips and dried in the sun ; it is an exceedingly
nourishing food, and, I am told, quite palatable.
Of course, the only possible way of eating it is to
slice it up into thin chips with a sharp knife, as it
is impossible to get your teeth through it otherwise ; a strip of it, to look at, is more like a
piece of very tough twisted wood than anything
else.

The transport of a commando, consisting of
waggons and teams of oxen or mules, was for
the most part commandeered by the authorities,
although some of the better class of burghers
brought their own waggons and Cape carts; and,
if one may judge from the contents of those
which we captured, they thought nothing of bringing half their household goods as well.   They were

Boer ox-waggons.

undoubtedly not worried with any field-service scale
limiting the weight of their personal baggage.

Many of their waggons contained huge iron bed-
steads, and it was not uncommon to come across the
incongruous sight of a bedstead lying in the open
veldt—thrown out, presumably, when the men were
hard pressed to lighten the load.

When the Boer travels he likes doing so in
comfort, and vast experience has made him an adept

at this. Every Boer farm has its equipment for travelling. The ox-waggon is the most generally adopted means of conveyance.

At least once or twice a year the Boer farmer proceeds with his family to the nearest town to attend nagmaal,[1] and he uses the same occasion in which to do any shopping and to transact his mercantile business.

Most of the Boer farming consists in cattle-raising; and thus for half the year, from June to November, the dry season in the low veldt, they are obliged to take their stock to the boschveldt. Naturally, with such continuous experience in travelling, the Boer knows the very best way to set about doing so. When transport was wanted, there was no difficulty in getting it. Every farm had its waggons and teams of oxen, or mules, and the Government had power to commandeer anything they required. An I O U, in behalf of the Government, would be given by the field cornet to the owners of any waggon and team required. How many of these I O U's were redeemed is another matter. It may be interesting here to note how the late Orange Free State branded their Government ponies. On the date specified

[1] Holy Communion.

in the commandier briif, the burghers would all appear on the market square of the dorp, or at the field cornet's farm, as the case might be, where they were formed up in line and a roll-call taken with a view to finding out the delinquents, if any.

So far the procedure of getting together a commando was identical with that for the mobilisation of our own reserves, with the difference, of course, that the reservist merely has to present himself at the appointed time and place, when his clothing and equipment, which is all ready waiting for him, is issued to him.

Orange Free State Government brand on pony.

My informant tells me that many of the burghers, in some cases actual sons of the soil, fled the country at the time of the outbreak of hostilities. Of course, as many Englishmen had become naturalised burghers, they had either to bear arms against their own countrymen or resort to this course to get out of so unlooked-for a contingency when they elected to take full burgher rights. I am not offering this explanation by way of an excuse. A man who voluntarily gives up his birthright should have considered every possibility before doing so.

After the roll-call the field cornet proceeded to inspect his commando, with the view of ascertaining what was wanted in the way of equipment. In many cases the burghers looked smart and business-like enough; but, on the other hand, the sight of some of the Taakhaar[1] Boers, I am told, would have caused a Trappist monk to forget his vows of silence. Picture to yourself the appearance of one man of the commando I am describing, whom his fellow burghers saw approaching the square. He presented a sight so ludicrous that he was received with good-humoured though derisive cheers. A raggedly-dressed man, mounted on a sorry nag that was only just able to drag its miserable carcase along, was slowly wending his way towards the assembled commando. On drawing nearer, his saddle was seen to consist of an old, empty, flour-bag; in place of stirrups, he had thrown a rope, looped at each end, over the bag; all that the bridle consisted of, and all that was apparently needed, was another rope thrown round the neck

[1] Longhair Boers, men from the up-country districts.

12

of his charger! It was eventually proved that the man was practically a pauper, living from hand to mouth; but, to his credit be it said, he

A Taakhaar Boer.

had done his best to comply with his commandier briif.

When the field cornet had finished his inspection, the burghers were informed of the station where they were to entrain and the time of their departure for the front. They were then left to look after themselves. No parade was ordered; there was no stirring band to accompany them down to the train; they usually arrived there in twos and threes, each man responsible for the entraining of his own horse, but all of them assisting at getting the waggons on to the trucks. This was no light matter; an ox-waggon built to withstand the South African roads being one of the most cumbersome and heavy vehicles imaginable, often weighing over thirty hundredweight and carrying a load of between four and five thousand pounds.

When everything was in readiness, amid much hand-shaking, waving of handkerchiefs, and God-speeds, with one warning whistle the train slowly steamed out of the station.

The scene at the station was pathetic, though boisterous. Each burgher's relations and friends being allowed on the platform, tear-stained faces were much more *en évidence* than at the many similar scenes at home.

The two Republics appear to have been very thoroughly divided up into separate districts; and over each of these districts, for the purposes of mobilisation, a general, or (to use the technical Boer term), a vecht-generaal, was appointed by the Government. The prefix 'vecht' (fighting) was used to show that the generaal so designated had a command at the front. The whole were under the supreme command of a Commandant-general. The destination of a commando would depend altogether on the position in the fighting line relegated to the vecht-generaal under whose command it was.

On arrival at the Hoofd-laager, or head-quarters encampment, the field cornet, after having been shown the position he was to take up, issued his orders for the pitching of the camp. The transport section was generally laagered in the rear of the combatant portion of the commando.

As soon as all the tents had been pitched and the transport laagered up, the assembly was blown by the commando bugler. (I should have mentioned that attached to each commando was the volunteer corps of the district from which it was formed.) The burghers by this time would begin to awake to the fact that they were no longer quite free to do as they pleased, and would have to submit to a certain amount of military discipline,—the assembly

having been sounded for the purpose of their hearing an address from their commandant, in which
he informed them of the fact that they were now
under 'Krijgs-Wet,' or martial law.   He told them
of the penalties for disobedience to their officers,

Boers listening to address by their commandant.

not complying with orders, sleeping on their post,
and any other matters which he considered relevant
to the discipline of the commando.

It would have been interesting to know what the
various penalties were ; but this I was not told.   I
have heard that one of the punishments resorted to

for a sentry sleeping on his post was to peg him down over an ant heap until he was stung to such an extent that nothing in the world would induce him to sleep on his post again. I can quite believe that this would be the effect of such a drastic measure; but I cannot vouch for the truth of the story. I should say that corporal punishment with the sjambok would be more likely.

After having carefully impressed all the burghers with the punishments they were to expect for any breach of discipline, the commandant would call for the election of non-commissioned officers. As a general rule a korporaal (corporal) was elected for every ten men of the commando, the burghers having absolute freedom to elect whom they pleased. No doubt this system of election worked well enough with the Boers, and was the only one that would have had a chance of succeeding among a people so self-reliant, and brought up from their infancy to such freedom of thought and action as they were. Presumably the only man who might wish to object to the election would be the corporal himself, the title his comrades had just conferred on him being by no means an empty one.

His duties were manifold and never-ending. He represented his section in everything, and had

to feed, clothe, and detail them for the various camp
duties that might fall to their lot.   We can picture
him at the end of the day declaiming loudly and
in no measured or uncertain terms at the popularity
among his comrades that
had brought him this high
but unwelcome honour.

The newly-fledged cor-
poral's first duty would be
to feed his ten men ; and
should the bill of fare of
the next section under, let
us say, Korporaal du Toit,
be better than that which
he had provided, each one
of the ten took no pains to
conceal the fact from him.
Then he had to requisition
for clothes.   They were not
particular, perhaps, as to the
cut of the breeches he had

A Boer.

drawn for them, and did not trouble themselves
much whether they were made by Tautz or an
Indian durzi ; but at least they did know what
cloth would stand rough usage and what would
not ; here again, possibly, Korporaal du Toit had

got the better of him, and it wasn't long before he was apprised of the fact.

To him fell the duty also of detailing his men for such duties as digging trenches, 'veld wacht,'[1] and, in connection with the commissariat department, helping in slaughtering the cattle and sheep for the commando. There were times when he might even have to act as chaplain-in-ordinary to his section.

Up to the capture of Pretoria the Boers in the field were well fed, and many luxuries were sent to the different commandos to supplement their ordinary rations. The articles of diet supplied daily as rations consisted of coffee and sugar, bread or meal if preferred, baking powder being included with the latter, fresh meat, always issued in the shape of live cattle or sheep, and in the way of vegetables potatoes and perhaps onions, also rice and pepper and salt.

Each section had to make its own arrangements for slaughtering and cutting up their cattle or sheep near the camp. In connection with this, here is an anecdote in the words of my informant:—

" It was always the rule that cattle or sheep were to be killed during the early hours of the morning,

[1] Sentry-go.

24   An early drink

25   Boer transport crossing a drift

as the slaughter-place was in sight of the British
guns, and it was their playful habit to throw a
few shells at the position during the day.   On this
particular morning some difficulty was experienced
in getting the cattle together to shoot the beast
selected.   It was rather late—past seven, I think
—when the ox was shot, and we were preparing to
perform the operation of skinning the carcase when
we heard a good deal of shouting from the camp to
the effect that the British had their guns in position
and were on the point of firing.   There was no
doubt about it: they did fire, but were aiming on
the position to our left.   We expected them to turn
their attention to us at any moment, and proceeded
with our work in feverish haste, and as fast as could
reasonably be expected from amateurs.   We were
not left long in doubt or peace.   The first shell in
our direction went screaming over our heads and
burst far behind us; the next fell a little to our
left; and, going on the old axiom that discretion
was the better part of valour, we left the half-
skinned carcase to its fate, and precipitately fled—
not a moment too soon, as the next shell ploughed
up the ground which we had just quitted.   As was
to be expected, the rest of the men in camp were
not particularly polite to us, the loss of fresh meat for

the day making them somewhat bitter and sarcastic ; many remarks which certainly were not complimentary, though perhaps merited—somewhat to the effect that we were better suited to starched linen than to the slaughter-yard—were freely hurled at us."

I happened to be present with our gunners at one of these little diversions ; on this occasion the Boers, probably spurred on by the jeers of their comrades, made several frantic efforts to carry off the carcase ; the amusement certainly was all on our side.

As may be well imagined, the state of the ground in the vicinity of a Boer camp of any standing was not pleasant. No attempt seems to have been made to bury the entrails of the slaughtered cattle, the Aasvogels [1] evidently being considered sufficient as scavengers.

Although there was practically no routine work for the commando in camp, there was, of course, always something to be done, and each section took it in turns. During an off-day the burghers did much as they pleased.

All the burghers and their officers slept near the entrenchments, so as to be in their places in

[1] Vultures.

case of an attack.   A general stir was made early in
the morning, when all blankets, pillows, etc., were
laid out to air.   As the majority of the Boers each
had a Kaffir boy as a servant, on rising in the
morning they were confronted with a steaming cup
of coffee.   The comfort of this on a cold winter's
morning in South Africa can only be realised by
those who have experienced what it is to be without
it.   After his morning coffee, a *sine quâ non* with
the burgher, he sauntered off to the tents to arrange
about breakfast; in the meantime the tents were
cleaned up, and everything was put straight.   If
the camp happened to be in the vicinity of a river
many of the burghers took a plunge before breakfast, though others, I am told, certainly did not
believe in cleanliness being near of kin to godliness,
and firmly protested against any such up-to-date
ideas.   Breakfast over, we have a picture of the
Boers squatting about in groups, under their
waggons or whatever shade was obtainable, smoking
and discussing the pros and cons of the war.

Each burgher had his own views on every
subject discussed, and often there were heated
arguments on the capabilities and military knowledge of their generals.   Modesty is not a character-
istic the Boers can lay claim to, and the want of it

is rather objectionable at times. I have come to the conclusion, however, that this lack of modesty is rather a good point in a soldier, if kept within reasonable bounds.   It certainly tends to self-

A morning discussion.

reliance.   It is far better he should think that he is capable of doing anything and everything as well as anyone else than to have the contrary opinion. I cannot, however, say that I should like to see this view generally adopted by ourselves: our mess and ante-rooms might become unbearable.

The Boers have the true love of sport bred in them, and this I consider the strongest reason for believing that they and we will become firm friends. They will always pride themselves on being able to beat you at any game; but show them that they have made a mistake, and they will be quick to recognise it.

The games with which they chiefly amused themselves on commando were quoits, blanket-tossing, and boxing. For the blanket-tossing, instead of an ordinary blanket, a specially-prepared cowhide was used, and the victim did not always have a very easy time; this occasionally led to an altercation which, if not taken in good part, most probably ended in a case of boxing in real earnest.

A favourite way of passing the time was to get up various kinds of boxing competitions. One form these took was, instead of putting on gloves, to use the flat of the hands; another was to try and remove a cap from the opponent's head; their own, naturally, coming in for a fair share of attention. Good temper and tact, however, were the rule. In their boxing such a thing as time is unknown. They go on until one or other of them throws up the sponge.

An event which was looked forward to by the Boers, just as much as by ourselves, was the arrival of the post. Their telegraph and field-post arrangements appear to have been very well managed. The Government also took good care to supply the different commandos with news of the war. This news, however, was 'untrue and misleading'; these are the words of the burgher to whom I am indebted for this account of their life. In another chapter I shall endeavour to show how untrue and misleading this news was.

A Boer was not allowed to leave his own commando to visit a neighbouring one, or the Hoofdlaager or headquarters of the commandant, without permission; there was no difficulty, however, in obtaining leave to do so. Before the capture of Pretoria leave of absence to visit their homes was granted to a certain percentage of the burghers; ten days or a fortnight at a time was the most they generally got. After our occupation of the capital this indulgence was not possible.

In the evening, if the burghers had not had a gloom cast over their camp through the death in action of one or more of their comrades, they all sat down to a convivial meal. Before this, however, the veldwacht had to be posted. When that had

been done and everything was quiet, fires would
be lit and the cooking-pots set going. The Boers
always carried their three-legged cooking pots with
them, slung, as a rule, under their ox-waggons.
These pots are the very best for camp life. You
have only to rest them on the ground, place a few
sticks between the legs, and light your fire: your
dinner will then cook without any fear of upset-
ting. During the earlier stages of the war, with
Pretoria behind them, the Boers were supplied
with many delicacies sent by relations and friends ;
but after the capture of the capital they had to be
content with very plain fare. One of the greatest
hardships at the end of the war was the want of
coffee and sugar, which are absolute necessities to
the Boers. Sardines were a favourite adjunct at
their dinner-table : this was evident from the
quantity of empty tins we found in the wake of the
Boer army. It is astonishing what a difference an
addition of this kind makes to one's ordinary fare.
For example, a little Worcestershire sauce with
bully-beef transforms an unappetising dish into quite
a delicacy. One of the few luxuries that I found
at Kroonstad immediately after our occupation of
the town was a supply of sauce—A1 Sauce, if I
remember rightly—and a few bottles of olives. I

secured these, though at the time I was really in quest of jam; nor did I regret having done so when I found out how greatly this sauce was appreciated afterwards, and what a difference it made to our meals.

The Boer system of outposts was not very elabo-

Kroonstad.

rate. However, they always had their cordon of sentries posted—to be detailed for veld wacht in winter being one of the duties most detested by the burghers. In summer this duty was not so trying —nothing could be lovelier than a cool, clear, summer's night in South Africa—but in winter it was a very different matter. After an intensely hot day no sooner has the sun disappeared over the

horizon than a sudden change sets in, and with the
rapidly growing darkness the warm day gives way
to a bitterly cold night.   It was not unusual on
waking up in the morning to find one's blankets
stiff with the frost, and water-bucket covered
with thick ice.   In South Africa twilight is unknown.   Night follows the day with extraordinary
rapidity, and unless it happens to be moonlight the
veldt is soon enshrouded in deep blackness.   Sentry-
go at night was always a trying duty : at no time
more so than the hour just before dawn.   The intense darkness, combined with the vastness of the
veldt, caused a weird feeling of loneliness ; the
slightest sound was magnified a thousand times
by the incessant strain of listening and watching ;
each object that with the coming dawn became
more and more clearly outlined against the sky-
line assumed the appearance of life, and, however
certain one might be that it was only imagination
tricking the susceptible brain, it was difficult to
convince oneself.   One can picture the burgher, a
silent watchful figure, imagining shadowy khaki
forms silently creeping from rock to rock, far off as
yet, perhaps, but stealthily getting nearer and
nearer, until the first faint gleam of dawn seems to
reveal to his overwrought brain the sudden glint

of the dreaded bayonets. "Halt! We gaan daar?
Allamagtach, et es de verdomde rooineks!"[1]   A
flash and report; yet another, and another, in rapid
succession; and our veldwacht has emptied his
mauser into the blackness before him.   Ere he can
place another clip of cartridges in his magazine the
whole commando is astir.   "The verdomde rooineks

A young Boer.

are on us!" is the one thought present in each
burgher's mind as, tumbling out of his blanket, he
snatches up his mauser and bandolier, and rushes
to his place in the trenches.   It is but the work
of a few seconds for every man in the commando
to empty clip after clip of cartridges until the dark
veldt is seamed and torn in every direction; but no
sound save the cracking of their mausers and hissing
of the bullets disturbs the stillness of the night.

[1] Rooinek (redneck), a contemptuous name for the British soldier.

Possibly it was only the coming dawn striking some blade of grass or rock, wet with the heavy dew, that had put the finishing touch to the burgher sentry's fevered imagination: the full dawn showed nothing more than the silent and lonely veldt.

There was a scene such as this at Paardeberg the evening before Cronje surrendered. The silence of the night was broken by the continuous roar of incessant rifle-fire. For the space of five or ten minutes every Boer trench was lit up by the frenzied flashes from the mausers, sweeping the ground in front of them with a deadly shower of lead. It was Cronje's last flicker. The little white flag showing above the trenches at dawn revealed the fact that after his plucky resistance he had recognised the inevitable and given up the hopeless struggle.

The Boers as a rule are very strict from a religious point of view, and never retire to rest without singing a hymn and offering up a prayer. It was very weird at night to hear the rough, untrained voices chanting the Psalms in various keys. A chaplain, or (to give the Dutch name) predikant, was attached to most commandos, and on Sunday services were held both in the morning and in the evening. When no predikant was procurable the service was generally conducted by some venerable old burgher.

The Boers are endowed with a sense of humour. A certain commando was amused by its predikant, who, having ferreted out a most convenient hiding-place, and constructed with much labour an elaborate bomb-proof shelter, so as to be far removed from the danger of bursting shells, emerged from his retreat each Sunday, and boldly walked into camp to hold his services. In no measured terms, and with all the vehemence he could command, he would then exhort them always to be brave and show a bold front to the enemy. Possibly some of his listeners were better acquainted than he presumably was with the well-known German proverb, " Good example is half a sermon."

From what we saw of the Boers in the field, I am sure it will be readily granted that in them we have the nucleus of an ideal army. Each burgher appeared to be able to grasp the situation, and work independently, without supervision, yet in conjunction with the others. Discipline and a better system of control seemed all that was necessary to make them one of the finest fighting

machines in the world. In their strength, however, lay their weakness. Their independence of
character was allowed too loose a rein. Apparently
the commando was the smallest unit reckoned with
for the purposes of fire discipline and control.
This is completely at variance with all our accepted ideas on this point. Though, as we have
seen, the commando was divided up into sections
of ten men, each under a corporal, this rank
carried with it no authority whatever. The
corporal was nothing more or less than an
orderly-man. The only time he assumed any
authority over his men was when his section
happened to be detached from the main body;
and then his authority was merely temporary.
No good result could possibly come from such
a system. However, the result which the Boers
did obtain served to show how marvellously self-
reliant and intelligent each individual burgher
in the commando must have been. I often
wondered how the burghers were controlled in the
firing line: each man appeared to have absolute
freedom to do as he thought fit, and concerted
action seemed impossible.

Their retirements were invariably begun by one
or two men galloping off, followed by others at

intervals.   Only when they had got well out of
range did we see them as a body; and then they
appeared more or less of an undisciplined mob.
From what I have since learnt, I gather that the
officers' control over their men was not great.
Each individual acted more or less on his own
initiative.   Had they been under control we should

Boers retiring.

no doubt have had a far harder task.   With
European nations depending to a great extent for
recruiting on their manufacturing towns, this state
of individual independence of thought and action
is out of the question.   We can, however, aim at
the ideal suggested by the imperfect system of the
Boers, and accomplish much by a systematic training of the young idea with this end in view.

THE FIELD POST

THE FIELD POST

I AM perfectly certain that for those who have not experienced what it means to be separated for weeks at a time from their mails, it is impossible to realise what this bugle-call meant to us who heard it on the veldt in South Africa. The words Tommy associates with it are these—

" A letter from your mother, Joey, Joey, Joey, Joey, Joey,

A letter from your mother, Joey, Joey, Joey, Joey, Joey."

Bugle-call : arrival of the post.

At any other time we should have considered

camp rendered hideous by every Tommy whose
lips were not too dry whistling this tune for all
he was worth, as the welcome call was taken up
and passed on to each unit by its respective
bugler.

This call has the same effect on me as the
refrain of Mark Twain's tram-conductor.—

> " A blue tip slip for a one cent fare,
>   A pink tip slip for a two cent fare.
>   Punch, brothers, punch ; punch, brothers, punch,
>   Punch in the presence of the passengare."

I do not vouch for the accuracy of this quotation,
as it is many years since I came across it. I well
remember, however, the baneful way in which
these words forced themselves upon me for a long
time afterwards.

Nevertheless, we looked forward to and welcomed this post-call as we did nothing else during
the war ; which surely is enough to show what a
feeling of good cheer the arrival of our mails
brought into camp. All praised the work done
by the Army Postal Corps in South Africa. We
were often bitterly disappointed at not receiving
our mails before trekking from any one place, not
knowing when or where we should have another

opportunity of getting them, and several times we lost them altogether; but these were from mishaps for which the Army Postal Corps were in no way to blame. My regiment had had hard luck at Sanna's Post. As mentioned in an earlier chapter, two days after the occupation of Bloemfontein, three companies were sent to occupy the water-works; three days later, on the 18th March 1900, the remaining company went with General French's Flying Column to Thabanchu, where we stayed until the 30th. Our mails, which we had not received for some time, had been accumulating, until we had as many as six weeks' due. On the morning of the 30th four bags of these arrived at Thabanchu, which we began to sort. Two bags had been opened and sorted, and, while this was going on, to help to pass the time I pulled out my sketch-book and had just pencilled in the little sketch, the frontispiece to this chapter, when a thunderbolt arrived in the form of an urgent message to inspan, saddle up, and await orders. The remaining two bags had to be put unopened on to one of the waggons, and we never set eyes on them again; they were captured by the Boers, with our convoy, at Koorn Spruit.

This, however, was not the full extent of our loss. The next morning, just as we were saddling up after the Boers had begun shelling our camp, a trooper of Roberts' Horse, who had arrived some time that night from Bloem-

fontein, having driven over in a Cape cart, came up to me and said, " I have brought two mail - bags from Bloemfontein for you, sir. What shall I do with them ? " " Throw them on to that waggon, please ; at any rate, they ought to get safely away," I answered, point-ing to our nearest transport waggon. Was there ever a worse forecast ? These waggons, as we all know, not many minutes afterwards were the very first to fall into the hands

One of Roberts' Horse.

of the Boers lying in ambush at the Koorn Spruit, and we had the mortifi-cation of seeing our long-looked-for mails lying such a short distance from us, yet hopelessly out of reach. If anything had been needed to spur us on to try and retrieve that disaster, it would have been the thought of those lost mail-bags.

One of my letters captured that day was sent to me months afterwards by a brother officer from Winburg, with a note saying that it had been picked up by Mr Darragh, who was then station-master there. It had been opened, of course, but carefully put back in the envelope. I should like to take the opportunity here of thanking my unknown Boer friend, who at any rate saved my letter—let us hope, on the chance of some day being able to restore it to its owner!

The next disaster to our mails occurred at Roodeval in June 1900. This was more serious. In addition to our letters, parcels, and papers, great quantities of winter clothing and comforts for the men were also lost. We in particular were most unfortunate in losing as much as we did, as we had just missed getting a portion of these mails when we left Bloemfontein in the general advance on May 1, and on reaching Kroonstadt heard that a quantity of mails for us had arrived at the former place, but that they would have to remain there for some time, as no room could be spared on the transport trains to bring them on. When they eventually were forwarded, De Wet managed to end their career and dash to the ground our hopes of ever seeing them, by capturing them with the convoy at Roodeval. The train which was conveying myself and a number of other sick officers from the hospitals at Pretoria to Cape Town on the way down stopped at the scene of this disaster. As it tarried some little time at Roodeval, we had ample opportunity of gauging the extent of the damage to our convoy, indication of the beginning of those numerous attacks by De Wet on our lengthened lines of communication which, emboldened by this success, he carried on so persistently. The scene was pitiful. For some considerable distance around the ruins of the station buildings the veldt was strewn with the charred remains of mail bags, burnt letters, papers, parcels of every description, warm clothing, and comforts for the troops, which were so badly needed at that time. The Boers, I was told, helped themselves to whatever they could carry away, and then burnt everything else. It went to one's heart to see the charred remains of British warm coats simply carpeting the veldt—a luxury which at that time could not be bought for love or money. To those who do not know what a British warm coat is, I should explain that it is a loose three-quarter length (to borrow a woman's descrip-

26   The Vet River fight as seen by the boers

27   Siege gun shells destroyed by De Wet

tion) slip-on overcoat, with many large pockets, the whole garment warmly lined with flannel. In a country where in winter a scorchingly hot day very soon after sundown is followed by a bitterly cold night, the tem-perature frequently falling as much as 50°, the comfort and use of a coat that is not too bulky to be strapped on to one's wallet, and therefore always getatable, can easily be imagined. In the high veldt the extremes of heat and cold are very great, the thermometer in winter fre-quently falling from 80° in the day to 20° at night.

A very curious experience happened to a brother officer on this train. While rooting about among the *débris* he

The British warm coat.

actually came across a portion of a burnt envelope addressed to himself. Although he searched for a long time, that was the only portion of the letter that he could find.

There were many evidences on all sides of the

stubborn fight at the railway station.   Boer shells
had plunged through the station water-tank,
smashed and overturned railway trucks, played
havoc with the railway-station building itself, and

The ruins of Roodeval railway station.

ploughed up the ground all round.   There remained
of the station sheds nothing but the foundations
and a few steel uprights, and of the goods trucks
the wheels and steel framework; the latter in
many instances being twisted and bent into every
distorted shape imaginable.   Near the railway
water-tank was lying a Milners' safe, the door of

which had been neatly blown out by the Boers in
the search for loot.   The rails had been torn up for
miles, the telegraph wires cut, and many of the
poles along the line pulled down.   A number of
immense siege-gun shells, battered and rent, lay
scattered about.   How the Boers managed to
destroy these I cannot say.

Our servants seemed keenly interested in these

Burnt-out trucks at Roodeval.

huge instruments of destruction.   They certainly
were rather awe-inspiring; personally I had never
seen anything like them before.

When one considers the enormous army we had
in South Africa, and the vast extent of country
over which it was spread, and recalls to mind
how impossible it was during the war to find out
the whereabouts of any particular body of troops,
let alone individuals, and the difficulties of knowing

how to address them, one begins to realise approximately what a stupendous task the Postal Corps must have had to cope with. I made a point of trying to find out somewhat how the work was carried on. Its magnitude was only too evident by one glance into the Field Post Office at Cape Town, where I went to try and secure my mails when on my way home. To ensure accuracy, an index register was kept, when possible, of the names of individuals in each unit, and against each name was entered the latest information of the whereabouts of the owner, gathered with immense trouble and labour from headquarters or from the units, even from the individuals themselves. On the arrival of a mail, it was first sorted into regiments, and then alphabetically; the addresses were then compared with those in the register, and amended where necessary. The number of letters requiring re-direction must have been enormous, as the best direction when in doubt, or in fact at any time, and the one most generally adopted, was, after the name of the individual's regiment, simply " Field Force, South Africa"; the rest was left to the Army Postal Corps. For an instance of the difficulty they must have experienced, one only has to consider for a moment that many of the companies in the mounted infantry regiments were composite companies.

My own regiment of four companies was made up of detachments from no fewer than eighteen different regiments; and as most of these regiments afterwards formed their own mounted infantry companies, which in their turn went to form new composite regiments of mounted infantry, the trouble and care necessary to unravel the whereabouts of any particular individual must have been enormous.   I believe the average army mail from home received at Cape Town during the war was over eighty bags of letters, about four hundred bags of newspapers, and from eight thousand to ten thousand parcels.   During the weeks preceding Christmas, this mail was often trebled and more than trebled.   One must certainly admire the system adopted by the Army Post Office in South Africa, which worked so well and successfully coped with the many difficulties that had to be encountered.

BRAVE WOMEN

BRAVE WOMEN

MOST of those who went through the South African campaign must have seen and admired the pluck, heroism, and marvellously unselfish love for their country which were shown by the Boer women. In saying this I do not wish it to be thought for one moment that, by only instancing and drawing attention to the bravery and heroism of the Boer women, I am detracting from or losing sight of the same qualities which our own countrywomen possess and were called upon to show in no smaller measure. No one could have been more tried, or have been asked to show these qualities in a higher degree, than the thousands of women who were brought face to face with the realities and horrors of war in Ladysmith, Kimberley, Mafeking, and in the numberless villages and farms in the Cape Colony and Natal; or those who had to bear their patient suffering and anxiety thousands of miles from the seat of war.

I do not attempt more than to give my impressions and experiences of a people who have now come under the British flag, a people who are unknown to the majority of their fellow-countrymen in other parts of the vast British Empire; and in doing so, perhaps, I may in a small way help to make them better known and understood.

The sufferings of our own people, patiently and nobly borne, are so fresh in our memories, and have been so forcibly brought home to us, that a better pen than mine is needed to add in the slightest degree to the honour and admiration which we all feel to be their due, or to make us recognise any the more that the little we went through was not one quarter as much as they were called upon to endure uncomplainingly.

We have been told again and again that it was the Boer women who kept the burghers at the front, the Boer women who encouraged and urged them on when encouragement was needed; in their unselfish devotion to their country, these women did not hesitate to brush all personal ties aside.

We all know what suffering was endured at

home, the intolerable suspense and dreary waiting for news, suspense long drawn out from days to months and perhaps years ; but put yourself in the place of these Boer women, who had actually to

Boer woman.

send off their husbands, brothers, or fathers, as the case might be, to fight often within sight of their own homes. Could anything have brought the possibilities and horrors of war more forcibly before them ?

What I am going to relate happened at a farmhouse not many miles to the west of Brandfort,
during our general forward movement from
Bloemfontein in May, 1900. I well remember
the instance, and I can still vividly see the pale,
agitated faces of these poor women. We were
sent off to work round a large kopje on our left
flank, which had been our objective the whole
day; the company forming the screen to our
movement had disappeared round the kopje, and
to all appearances it was not held by the Boers.
Noticing a farmhouse and Cape cart at the foot of
it, I obtained leave to ride up and inspect them.
At the first glance I saw unmistakable signs of
Boers having recently been there and of having
been disturbed. There was abundant evidence of
this in the fresh hoof-marks and bundles of oat-hay
scattered about the farmyard, barely half consumed.
I rode up to the house itself and questioned two
women who came to the door; but, of course, I
could obtain no information from them. They
declared they had seen no one, and that no Boers
had been near the place. Judging, however, from
the haggard looks and agitation of these women,
evidently mother and daughter, I felt certain that
they were trying to hide something. The wretched

mother was intensely nervous and agitated, and the girl had a wet handkerchief bound round her head and the most beseechingly haunted look in her eyes. Very soon I found out the reason. Hardly had I left the door when I heard the ominous click-clock of the mauser. The Boers were holding the kopje, and had opened fire on our scouts, whom they had allowed to get round and work close up to the far side of it.

Immediately I got my men behind the best cover I could, which was an empty dam at the side of the house, and from there we covered the retirement of the advanced company. It wasn't a place I should have chosen amid any other circumstances, as the kopje commanded us, and very soon our horses began to be hit, though we wedged them in behind us as closely as we could. However, it was the best cover obtainable, and it served to extricate our scouts from a nasty position.

Now, if you are able, try and realise the feelings of these poor women in the farmhouse close by. I have no doubt that the father and probably the brothers or the girl's sweetheart were on that kopje. At any minute these men might have met their death in full view of their home.

I will admit that had the latter been in the dam,

and we on the kopje, their grounds for fear would have been very much increased; but that is not the point.

To add to the horror of it for these women, when our guns came up, the kopje was shelled, and each shell as it hissed its deadly message over that farmhouse must have struck terror into their hearts.

The Boers eventually had to retire; and as we swept on, the thought of the tragedy that may have happened there was soon driven out of our minds by more work in front. As we passed I rode up to the farmhouse again, and was thankful to find that no harm had befallen the two women. After we had left, you can imagine with what feverish haste and dread they must have scrambled up that stone-faced hill—let us hope, to find that their fears were groundless.

We have all heard, I am sure, of the devoted and unselfish work of our own hospital nurses, and I don't think too much ever could be said in their praise. Of the Boer Red Cross nurses, however, I have seen no mention; yet how many of us owe to them a debt of gratitude, and possibly our lives?

When carried into Pretoria it was my good

fortune to get one of the two vacant beds in the
Bourke Hospital, for which I have to thank Civil
Surgeon Willis, who was in medical charge of us at
the time. This hospital was under the management
of Dr Veal, an English doctor resident at Pretoria
— whether a burgher or not I am unable to say.
His assistant was a German, and with them they
had a staff of Boer Red Cross nurses.

We had taken over the hospital on our occupation of Pretoria, and the nurses without a single
exception elected to remain and continue their
work of mercy.

At the time I was in the hospital it was about
half-full of Boer sick and wounded, the remaining
beds being allotted to us. Many of the Boers
appeared to be of a very rough up-country type;
but they were quite friendly, and showed no resentment at our occupation of their capital.

The nurses were amateurs—with the exception
of the matron, of whom everyone spoke in terms
of endearment and praise. They were all daughters
of leading families in the Transvaal. My nurse
told me that on the outbreak of hostilities they
went through a two-months course of regular
nursing.

The ward I was in was in charge of Sisters Estelle

Raymond and Friede König, and I am sure none of us will ever forget these bright, cheery little sisters; they seemed indefatigable, and we could never make out when they rested. Nothing could have exceeded their kindness or the thoroughness of their nursing. What an ideal nurse, too, was Miss du Plessis! She had a charm of her own that was bound to cheer any patient. How often, after sitting up all night with a delirious and dangerous enteric case, a ray of sunshine was brought into our ward, as she came in and with a bright smile wished us all a hearty good morning! She happened at the time to be doing night duty and to be nursing an officer well known to several of us in the ward, and a great favourite. He had practically been given up by the doctors; but Miss du Plessis each morning told us all her hopes and fears, and how she meant to save him. "He must—he shall—get over it," she said, and I shall not forget with what pride and pleasure she burst into our room one morning, to say that the crisis was over and that her patient was on the mend.

Careful nursing was all that was needed now, and the devoted lady certainly gave him that, and to her nursing he owes his life. She was always so cheerful and bright that someone asked her one

day what she thought of the war and how she
managed through it all to maintain such wonderful
spirits? She made a pathetic answer. "O, don't
talk to me of the war! It is bitterer than death
to me to lose our country; but I forget all this in
my nursing."

In charge of another ward, or rather wards, I
should say, as each of the sisters had several to
look after, were the two Misses Burgers. They
looked so frail that one could hardly picture them
going through all the hardships of a hospital
training. They were the daughters of the late Mr
Burgers, who was President of the Transvaal in
1877, when the country was annexed by Sir
Theophilus Shepstone. He took up his residence
in the Cape Colony, after entering a formal protest
against the annexation, and was pensioned by the
British Government.

I think I am right in saying that another of the
nurses was Miss Lucas Meyer, daughter of the
late General Lucas Meyer, whose sad death last
year, when nearing the end of his visit to this
country, provoked such deep and widespread
sympathy.

Another of the nurses—whose name, I am sorry
to say, I have for the moment forgotten (her father

was a resident of Pretoria, a Scotsman by birth, I
believe)—told me that, with only a small staff to
help her, she had taken several trips in charge of
a Boer hospital train, after the battle at Colenso.
What this meant, only those who have had any
experience of carrying the sick and wounded from
a battlefield and field hospitals to the base can

Boer hospital train.

realise.   She told me that she had an uncle serving
at the front with our Army Medical Corps, and,
by a curious coincidence, he was doing duty on
the very hospital train that took me down to
Cape Town.

I had hoped that the services of the Boer Red
Cross nurses, who during the war so nobly and
unselfishly tended our sick and wounded, not only
before the occupation of Pretoria—many officers

who were taken to Pretoria as prisoners of war came under their care—but afterwards also, would have been publicly recognised, and had some material token of recognition awarded them. If this, as I believe, has not been done, they at all events have won the admiration and gratitude of all who passed through the Bourke Hospital. I mention the Bourke Hospital because it was the only one that I had any experience of. I have no doubt that there were many other Boer Red Cross nurses just as deserving of our gratitude and praise.

To those of us who had the painful duty of searching Boer farms, numbers of which were found to be nothing but arsenals and granaries, many pathetic scenes must have presented themselves. These farms were invariably left in charge of the women and children, and one can well imagine how they must have hated the sight of us. An incident now to be recounted serves as a fitting illustration of the heroic spirit of the women. It was told to me by an officer of an irregular corps, at the close of a day on which we had been ordered to search a number of farms in a surrendered district south-east of Bloemfontein.

It fell to his lot to search a large farm which, I believe, belonged to the field cornet of the district.

I don't remember the reason why, but, at any rate, in accordance with one of the various Proclamations issued on the subject of the liability of farms to this penalty, this particular farm was ordered to be burnt. All the furniture that could be taken was removed from the condemned building by the troops, and then, while the dense black columns of smoke arose, and the hungry flames crackled and leapt from basement to roof of her home, what do you think this field cornet's wife did? I am perfectly certain that not one in a thousand would guess aright. She did not give way to hysteria— she was far too brave a woman for that—but sat down and made coffee for this officer and his men, at the same time saying, "I know you are only doing your duty as my husband is doing his." Such a high sense of duty, and such an undaunted spirit of self-sacrifice, is surely unparalleled in the history of any nation. The race that can boast of such women may well be proud.

This incident has brought in the vexed question of farm-burning. I don't wish to be led into a controversy on such a painful subject; but so many harsh and wild words have been used, by people obviously unacquainted with the Boer methods of fighting, and means of prolonging the struggle, and

also quite ignorant of the reasons which at times
made these actions imperative and necessary,
though utterly distasteful to all concerned, that I
cannot pass from the subject without saying,
though this should hardly be necessary, that the
women living on these farms were always treated
with the utmost consideration.   As much of their
furniture and personal belongings as possible was
invariably taken out of the condemned portion of

Boer farm.

the farm, and stored in the building left for them
to live in.

As an instance of the way in which well-edu-
cated people mislead the more ignorant on this
matter, I will give an extract from a letter of Miss
Olive Schreiner which was read at a meeting
of South African women at Somerset East in
Cape Colony :—

"That the bulk of the people of England could
sit silent and unmoved while private houses were

burnt down and women and young children turned homeless into the wilds, in order that through wounding the affections and sympathies of the men their army might be paralysed for further warfare . . . . had one told me that these things could be, and the bulk of the English nation sit by silent and unmoved, I would have regarded him as one who dreams in a fever."

I don't know whom we should pity the more —those who can stultify their reason to such an extent as to believe such things of their countrymen, or those ignorant people who are led into such a belief by these hysterical shrieks.

"Through wounding the affections and sympathies of the men their arms might be paralysed for further warfare."

Could anything be further from the truth, or show a more complete and miserable lack of ability to grasp the *raison d'être* of our action than the words I have just quoted ?

I can give one more instance that should rank high among the many individual acts of bravery that the war brought forth.

My heroine is Miss Back, the stepdaughter of a farmer who was a corporal in Methuen's Horse in 1885. Her home is in the Northern Transvaal.

28   A boer vrouw

29   A swarm of locusts

The incident occurred at the engagement at
Koster River on July 22, 1900, during an attempt
by Colonel Airey, commanding the 1st New South
Wales Regiment, to dislodge the Boers from a
position commanding the road between Stand's
River and Magato Nek.

Miss Back was in a farmhouse round which
there had been a good deal of the fighting. One
of the Queensland bushmen was wounded near
the house, and, seeing him lying there, she went
out and bandaged his wounds and carried him
inside. Her next thought was how to get a doctor
for him.

Borrowing a horse and saddle from another
trooper, she rode, under a heavy fire, to Colonel
Airey to ask him to send a doctor to the farm.
This Colonel Airey was unable to do, as the only
doctor with the force was himself wounded. Miss
Back then volunteered to ride on a man's saddle
to Magato Nek to try and get another. This,
however, was unnecessary, as someone had already
been despatched for one. Then, under fire, she did
all she could in the way of tending and dressing
the wounded. Next day she returned with lint
and bandages in case they should be required. On
her way to Colonel Airey Miss Back was repeatedly

shot at, and she had to walk part of the way under heavy fire. In attending to the wounded her conduct was still more heroic, as she had to do so between the Boers and Colonel Airey's party, and was consequently in the direct line of fire. The Boers paid a tribute to this heroism when they afterwards visited the farm where Miss Back was staying. Although suspicious that she had carried despatches, recognising her courage they treated her with every consideration. A thrill of pride should run through every woman who reads this story of simple heroism by one of their own sex.

SOME LEAVES FROM MY SKETCH BOOK

SOME LEAVES FROM MY SKETCH BOOK

"How did you manage to find time to make all your sketches?"

I have so often been asked this question that perhaps it would not be out of place here to explain.

To begin with, I invariably carried a sketch book in my haversack and one in my saddle-bags, so that

A commandeered ambulance.

I always had a book handy when an opportunity presented itself. It became almost second nature to me to jot down anything that interested me at the moment. When others, perhaps, were

233

lighting their pipes, or perchance taking a siesta,
I employed my time in attempting to transfer the
nearest scene to paper.   Of course, many incidents
that would have been by far the most interesting
to myself I was unable to sketch at the time.
Of one or two of these I kept some record by

General French's headquarters.   Koedoesrand.

pencilling in the scene while still pictured fresh
in my mind's eye.

The little farmhouse sketched above was used
by General French as his headquarters at Koedoesrand Drift.   It seemed quite a palace to us at the
time.   The farther belt of trees delineates the
banks of the Modder River, in which we found
an excellent bathing-place.

The sketch opposite was also made at the same

place. The river makes a sharp bend just below the kopje on the right, which is the Koedoesrand. The Kimberley-Bloemfontein road skirts this ridge, and the drift is at the foot of it. Cronje's laager was situated directly over the buck waggon, about five miles down the river.

Koedoesrand will ever be associated by those

Our field hospital, Koedoesrand.

who were there with rain and thunder storms. Day after day and night after night our men were drenched to the skin. These storms had the peculiar faculty of coming on us from one direction, and no sooner had they passed over and the rumbling of the thunder died away in the distance than, faint at first, but rapidly swelling in volume, the angry muttering of approaching thunder was again borne down on us from exactly the opposite quarter; and soon the whole storm burst over us afresh.   The rushing wind, bending everything low in its track, the deluge of rain, the blinding light- ning, and the crash of the thunder reverberating and echoing back from kopje to kopje, defied descrip-

Field-service kit packed for a storm.

tion.   There was one night which I shall never forget.   Several of us were sleeping under a rough shelter which we had formed out of a buck waggon- cover.   A thunderstorm of exceptional severity broke directly over us.   In an instant the shelter was bodily lifted up and hurled to the ground. This left us exposed to the full fury of the storm, without even waterproof sheets to protect us. The blankets soon were wet through, and we found ourselves lying in a pool. The whole veldt around had been converted into a lake when the storm had passed. After waiting some time to make sure that it was not returning, I got a change of clothing out of my saddle-bags; but, to my dismay, no sooner had I put them on than I heard the unmistakable distant rumbling of thunder. There was no doubt about it: the storm *was* returning. It came up with alarming rapid-

Trooper of the New Zealand M.R.

ity; and soon I was in a sorrier plight than ever with my only other suit of clothing soaked.

Another day also is strongly impressed on my mind. We were bathing when one of these storms broke overhead. Nothing could have been better as far as we were concerned, as we found sufficient cover under the river bank to shelter our clothes, and remained in the river until the storm was over. When we reached our bivouac, however, we found that a tragedy had occurred. The lightning had claimed a victim. A gunner had been struck and was being buried a few yards from our mess shelter.

This stalwart trooper overleaf, sketched while on forage fatigue at Koedoesrand, was one of the fine New Zealand Mounted Riflemen. During the advance to Pretoria we had the good fortune to be associated with this corps, the Queensland M.I., the Australian M.I., the 1st and 2nd Canadian M.R., Roberts' Horse, and Rimington's Guides ; as splendid a representative body of men as our colonies can produce and as one could wish to see. Nothing brought home to us the resources of the Empire more than these magnificent corps.

The Canadians, perhaps, were the most showy troops. They were men of immense physique, splendidly mounted and perfectly drilled.

Throughout the Boer war each one of these corps has earned a name for itself, and the Empire, that will for all time add lustre to the annals of the British army.

30   Colonel Rimington and some of his guides

31   Ambulances at Wynberg railway station

THE FALL OF BLOEMFONTEIN

After their obstinate and stubborn resistance at Driefontein on March 10 we quite expected

A group of Canadian M.R.

that the Boers would offer a strong opposition to the capture of the capital of the Orange Free State. With this idea we resumed our march next morning, bivouacking that night at Doorn-boom, a few miles south of Rep Kop. The whole of the next day General French pushed on, with a brief halt at Venter's Vlei, working south of the broad expanse of hills lying to the west of Bloemfontein. We passed all these ridges without any attempt being made by the Boers to retard our

Rep Kop.

advance, and began to think that perhaps, after all, the capture of the capital might not be seriously disputed. The farms conspicuously flying white flags lulled us into a feeling of security.

At about five in the afternoon we were rudely disillusioned. As we reached a point opposite Steyn's farm (a brother of the President's),

at the door of which a Cape cart was drawn up—
Mr Steyn being caught as he was about to make a
hurried departure—a puff of smoke on the railway
about a mile south of the farm, and right under the
upstanding Leeuwberg Kopje, followed by the
report of an explosion, at first I took to be a shell
bursting ; but no—it was the line south of Bloemfontein being blown up by us, the first sign of any
active operations during the day.

At the same moment, on our left, a galloper,
tearing back in all haste with a message for
General French, told us that the reconnoitring
squadron had obtained some information of
importance, which was immediately confirmed
by rifle fire on that flank.   Prompt as ever, the
whole machinery of the column was set in motion.
Roberts' Horse were sent off at a gallop to occupy
some low-lying kopjes on our left, while my company was sent forward to seize a kopje east of the
railway and directly over the Leper location.

Dashing forward, but keeping a little to the
south, so as not to be exposed to fire from the
kopje in case there was any difficulty in crossing
the railway, the scouts whom I had sent out at
a gallop reached this point.   I saw them all
dismount and come to a standstill.   What was

the matter? Every second's delay might be of the utmost importance. Spurring on my horse, I found that they had been stopped by a thick wire fence, forming an impassible barrier. I tried to sever this with my wire cutters; but these were perfectly useless. Though they had never failed me before, here I could make no impression whatever on the wire.

Impatient at the delay, I scattered my men along the line to the right and left in the hope of finding a weak spot somewhere, when by an extraordinary chance I came across an axe lying at the side of the rails. With this we quickly cut our way through. Then we raced for the kopje, reaching it only just in time, for as we swarmed up its steep boulder-faced side a few Boers who had also been racing for the same vantage point wheeled about and galloped off on the far side.

Facing us about 1500 yards distant was a long low ridge running east and west. From this a feeble attempt was made to bring a rifle fire to bear on to us. Their attention, however, was soon drawn off us by a squadron of Scots Greys who crossed the line below us, and, under a heavy outburst of firing from this ridge, galloped up the valley between. The evening was rapidly closing in, and in the dusk they disappeared. The firing soon ceased. The Greys had seized the ridge.

The Boers, who, from a kopje west of the line, had brought a pom-pom into action, kept up the shelling until late at night. They directed their fire chiefly on to a dam, the only place at which our horses could be watered. Our horse gunners replied, and this artillery duel in the dark was a pretty sight. First there was the flash from the Boer gun on the ridge, followed by a line of little spitting balls of fire in the veldt below; then the answering flash from our guns, the crest-line of the Boer position lit up for an instant as our shrapnel, with a bright flash and sharp report, scattered its bullets over the face of the hill. We were left undisturbed on our kopje, and employed our time in erecting sangars as a protection from the shelling expected at dawn.

The squadron of Scots Greys had secured a firm footing on the ridge in front of us; but it was a very extended position to hold with so few men, and they did not know what the morning might reveal. I met an officer galloping back for rein-forcements, which would have been sorely needed had the Boers attempted to dislodge this small force.

At daybreak we saw General French pushing

on beneath us, with some guns, to this ridge.
We followed, and from the crest-line saw Bloemfontein snugly lying in the valley below, only
about two or three miles from us. The Boer
gun that had annoyed us the night before could
be seen making off by a road running behind
the long flat ridge overhanging the town on the
north. Shortly afterwards I was sent forward

U Battery R.H.A. in position
before Bloemfontein.

with two companies of mounted infantry as an
escort to U battery, horse artillery, which had
taken up a position on a kopje to the south-east
and immediately over the Kaffir location, with
their guns grimly trained on the town lying at
their mercy not more than 2000 yards below.
The Boers had their revenge a little over two
weeks later, when this battery bore the full
brunt of our disaster at the Koorn Spruit ambuscade.

All firing had ceased, and we waited for the next move. That was to be either the surrender or the bombardment of the town, which had been given until twelve o'clock to decide.

A crowd of chattering, laughing natives, greatly excited, swarmed up from the location beneath us, examining the guns with awe-struck curiosity and uttering extravagant expressions of delight.

At about twelve o'clock a small khaki-clad column was seen leaving the ridge seized by the Scots Greys the evening before, and leisurely wending its way towards the town. This was Lord Roberts, accompanied by an escort of cavalry and mounted infantry. The keys of the capital had been handed over. Bloemfontein was ours. One more company of mounted infantry was sent for to join the procession, and I took mine, and was ordered to post pickets on all the exits to the town.

Instead of sullen, downcast faces awaiting us as we passed under the fort and entered the capital, we met with a most enthusiastic welcome. An excited crowd lining the route cheered again and again. Women and children, decked with red-white-and-blue rosettes and ribbons, crowded round us waving handkerchiefs amid all possible

manifestations of delight. Could this be the
surrendered capital of the Free State, or was it all
a dream from which we should be awakened by
the screeching of a shell, to find ourselves on a
lonely sangar-crested kopje, the sport of the
Boer guns? No. That warm shake of the hand
was real. We were indeed treading the streets
of Bloemfontein.

The long-stifled feelings of these people (the
town seemed peopled with English) broke out in a
warm-hearted welcome the like of which we never
met with in any other part of South Africa.
Women and children pressed forward, and enthusi-
astically shook us by the hand. "Our mouths
have been shut for months," one said to me.
"We cannot restrain our feelings any longer.
We have been living in a reign of terror, and
had but to bestow a friendly smile on the
English prisoners of war passing through on
their way to Pretoria, to feel a tap on the
shoulder and be told that our names had been
noted. The next warning would be in the form
of an order to leave the town within twenty-four
hours, and be put across the border."

I hadn't been standing on the market square five
minutes before one Dutchman after another came

up and asked me to go to the nearest hotel and have a drink. I should not have remarked on this had not the behaviour of these same men a few days later, as I noted in a previous chapter, been of a very different character.

One man followed me about protesting that he had not been fighting, pulling out a red-cross badge. "See! I have only been with the ambulances," he said. I could not help retorting: "Well, if you were not fighting for your country, you should have been."

The German portion of the population were bitter, and made no attempt to hide their feelings. When, after our disaster at Sanna's Post, I was sent to Cape Town to obtain supplies and kit to take the place of those which we had lost, obliged to pass the night in Bloemfontein, I asked for a bed at the Free State Hotel. "You may sleep on the stoep," was the answer of the German proprietor.

My journey to Cape Town reminds me of an ingenious Boer trap which I saw from the train on my return journey, at the Oorlogs Spruit, a few miles north of Colesberg Junction, guarding the culvert over the spruit, which was in rear of the Boer position at Colesberg, from any attempt on our part to blow it up.

Approached from Colesberg (which is beyond the far ridge), the loopholed embankment could not be detected. It merely merged itself into and appeared to be a continuation of the far side of the Spruit. It was only when one had passed it and looked back that one saw the ingeniousness of this

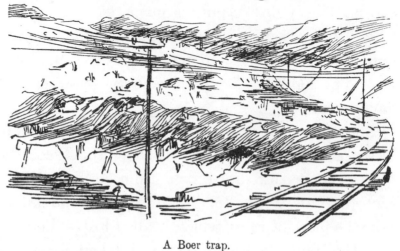

A Boer trap.

Boer trap, with the Spruit behind as cover for their ponies and a safe retreat for themselves. I do not think that any attempt was made by us to blow up this culvert.

THE ZAND RIVER

On May 7, the Boers, retiring before our advance, took up a position across the Zand River at Virginia Siding. As we, following close on the heels of their rear-guard, having had three encounters with them within four days, reached Welgelegen Siding, about eight miles south of this, a dense column of smoke, followed by a dull report, suddenly shot up in front of us. This was the Zand River railway-bridge being blown up. We did not proceed, but bivouacked at this siding, and had scarcely off-saddled when an order was received to saddle-up again. With barely time to tighten up our girths, the whole brigade, under General Hutton, was cantering along the side of the line toward the Zand River.

Wild rumours were rife as to what we were going to do. The general impression was that the Boer convoy had come to a deadlock while attempting to ford the river. When we got to the end of a rise overlooking it, the whole Boer army was seen to be comfortably encamped on the far side of the river. Waggons were laagered up, fires lit; and there was not a sign of anything amiss. We came to a standstill, and with field glasses glued to our eyes stared at the scene opened out before us not more than two miles in front.

This was too good an opportunity to be missed by the Boer gunners. Astounded, at first, at our audacity, they quickly pulled themselves together

and turned on to us every gun they possessed.
Their big guns were mounted on railway trucks,
and from this position we could plainly see them
bringing them into action. Shell after shell came
hissing towards us, and, with dull thuds as they
struck, tore up the ground on all sides. Still we
sat stolidly and looked on.   At length the order to
retire a few hundred yards was given. As we turned
about, a shrapnel from one of their big guns burst
with a deafening crash directly over my company.
There was a regular shower of bullets. They
struck the ground on all sides; but only two men
were hit, and beyond the denting-in of a cartridge
or two in their bandoliers no harm was done. Presumably the shell was burst too high. Once again
it was plainly demonstrated to us how ineffectual
the Boer shell-fire was. The majority of the shells
either buried themselves in the ground without
bursting, or else were burst too high.

We rode back the six miles to our bivouac,
feeling that we had given our tired ponies an extra
twelve miles on top of a long day for nothing.

Next day we had a rest, and only a short march
of eleven miles the day after, when we crossed the
Zand River at Du Preez Laager Drift, about twelve
miles west of Virginia Siding, and bivouacked on

the right bank, once more joining the 1st Cavalry Brigade. From Bloemfontein to Welgelegen the Mounted Infantry under General Hutton had formed the left column of the advance.

Our forward march was continued early next morning. As support to the 1st Cavalry Brigade

A Burmese pony.

we moved parallel with the railway about five miles west of it. Lord Roberts was marching directly up the line, while General Ian Hamilton was on the east of it. We reached the Dirksburg diamond mines without any sign of the enemy; but almost immediately after reaching this point we were ordered forward at a gallop, to take up a position

on some rising ground to cover our right flank.   A
few Boers were seen hurriedly riding off.   A certain
group of three I particularly noticed, as one of them
was unmounted and the other two appeared to be
trying to carry him off against his will.   No
sooner had we opened fire on them than the two
mounted men galloped off, and the third man
began to run towards us, throwing his arms about.
Then, pulling out a red handkerchief, he wildly

The Dirksburg diamond mines.

waved this above his head and reeled like a
drunken man.   It was quite evident that he was
wounded, and I sent two men out to help him in.
Watching him with my glasses as he got nearer, I
saw that he was one of our men.   He turned out
to be an Inniskilling dragoon whom the Boers
had wounded and were endeavouring to drag off
when we arrived on the scene.

The remainder of the day was spent in following
up the rear-guard of the Boer army, now in full

retreat. Later we saw them all streaming off towards Kroonstad—a medley of waggons, guns, and men.

Soon after passing the Vredeverdrag ridge, where a squadron of Inniskillings and Scots Greys shortly before had lost heavily, I saw a boy of not more than fifteen or sixteen years of age trying to conceal himself in the hollow of an old ant-heap. On

Action at the Zand River.

going up to him I found that he was badly wounded. Lifting him out, I sent back word to our ambulance. To my astonishment, he told me that his name was Elliot, that he was English, and that his parents were residents of Johannesburg. He had been ridden down in a charge by our cavalry. I believe the poor little fellow afterwards died of his wounds.

I was in command of our advance guard at the time, and could not but admire the tenacious way in which the Boer guns hung on to position after position during this rear-guard action.

The Boers are adepts at fighting a rear or flank-guard action ; and the conformation of the country afforded them every assistance. Not hampered by unmounted men, they were enabled to delay us and hang on to each successive position, with the whole of the force composing their rear-guards,

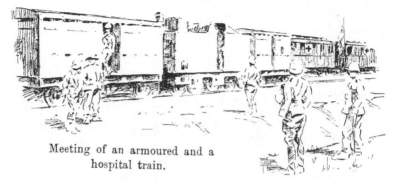

Meeting of an armoured and a hospital train.

until the last moment. They were also able rapidly to extend their position to either flank, to forestall any attempt at a turning movement on our part, and to deceive us as to their real strength.

Anyone who has studied military history will be able to recall many instances where a mere hand-ful of intelligent men acting in this way, with a resourceful commander, have kept a whole army at bay.

I can recall several such instances in the Boer war.

At Poplar Grove we were delayed by a small force operating on our right flank, while the whole Boer army retired across the open veldt not more than three or four miles ahead.   It is absurd, however, to think, as many critics have maintained, that our cavalry were thereby prevented from charging the retreating Boers.   I believe any cavalryman will tell you that this was an impossibility under the circumstances.   They had been in the saddle since three in the morning and covered close on forty miles, whereas the Boer ponies were fresh and lightly equipped.   Possibly the one or two guns with their rear-guard might have been captured; but they had before this secured the safe retirement of their waggons and big guns.   They actually attempted to charge our guns that day.   To turn their flank guard out of the position which they had taken up on our right, Colonel Alderson, with the Household Cavalry, two guns, and the Mounted Infantry, was ordered to seize some kopjes on our right rear.   As soon as we began to retire to do this, the Boers mounted their ponies and charged straight at our guns.   It was the work of a moment for the latter to unlimber and come into action with case shot. The Boers wheeled round, scattered, and fled.

Another successful rear-guard action was the covering of their retirement from the hills north of Brandfort over the Vet River. Kalkheuvel, on June 3, 1900, affords another instance. Du-Toit's retreating commando in the evening of that day successfully got their convoy away; but here, certainly, the nature of the country afforded him every assistance. What more favourable ground could be found for a rear-guard action?—though by saying this I don't wish it to be thought that I am in any way disparaging the plucky and gallant way in which the Boers fought these covering actions.

ENCOURAGING THE ENEMY

"FOUR HOSTILE NEWSPAPERS ARE MORE TO
BE FEARED THAN A THOUSAND BAYONETS."
—*Napoleon.*

ENCOURAGING THE ENEMY

THAT the Dutch as a nation before the war had no love for us we all know, and that they had been taught from their cradles to despise and hate the verdomde Englander we also know; but how this hatred was fostered and kept alive needs some explanation, as do the reasons that led many of the Colonial Dutch to throw in their lot with the Republics.

Their minds, in the first place, were inflamed by Dr Leyds, working through the continental press; but also for a further explanation we have not to go so far afield — we must look at home. During our advance to Pretoria, what did we find in every town and many of the farms throughout the Free State and the Transvaal? English pro-Boer papers, or excerpts from them reprinted in the Dutch papers; and we found them not only reprinted in the Transvaal and the Orange Free State, but also in the very heart of Cape Colony itself.

To an ignorant people who firmly believe that whatever they see in print must necessarily be true, the statements contained in these papers served to "make assurance doubly sure," to corroborate the loathsome and foul lies spread broadcast throughout South Africa by the continental press.

It is easy enough, and requires no stretch of imagination, to gauge what would be the effect, on the minds of a people ignorant and already embittered against us, of statements such as these, made not only by many influential people in this country, but also by some of the most prominent members of the Opposition in the House of Commons.

We know that they read the speeches of these men, reported to have been made before densely packed audiences, who were said to have cheered the speakers to the echo,—speeches to the effect that it was an unjust and cruel war, a war carried on by methods of barbarism and wanton cruelty, and, as a culmination to these shrieking utterances, the hint or prophecy that the Government only had to be defeated to put an end to the war. If the Dutch saw these speeches reprinted once, they saw them a hundred times, and each time with heightened colour.

I was told by a resident at Kroonstad that an ex-M.P.—an Irishman, I regret to say—had, the evening before we entered the town, held a crowded meeting of burghers, and urged them not to be disheartened, but to continue the struggle. Time, he said, would give them the victory, and free them from the Saxon oppressor. Surely no one could have despised this man more than the Boers themselves.

These same papers and men cried out that the concentration camps, to put it bluntly, were nothing but death traps formed for the sole purpose of enabling us to exterminate the Boers, by killing all the women and children. Shrieking English-women inspected these camps and cried out in horror at the cruelty of them, and the pestilential state they were in. Happily, we have not only the Boer women themselves, but the Dutch parsons also, who were in these camps, to give such statements the lie direct.

We come here to a question as to how far liberty of speech should induce criticism on the policy of a Government when once that Government has committed the nation to a war. Surely there can be no two opinions on this point. To me, at least, it appears that it is the bounden duty of every subject in the nation to stand by that nation until at least the war has ended, and that any criticism, or crusade against the Government, tending to give encouragement to her enemies to prolong the war, should be treated as treasonable.

Sedition, among other things, consists in the " bringing into hatred or contempt, or exciting disaffection against, the Sovereign or the Government, or in raising discontent and disaffection among his Majesty's subjects, or in promoting feelings of ill-will and hostility between different classes of such subjects." But then there comes a saving clause— " A person is not guilty of sedition who acts in good faith, merely intending to point out errors or defects in the government." After reading this definition of sedition, what doubt can there be in anyone's mind that many of the speeches made throughout the war would have been treated as treasonable had not the speakers been saved by this last clause? My contention, however, is that when a man finds that, by pointing out in all good faith what he may consider errors or defects in the government, he is doing incalculable harm and otherwise causing the same effect that a treasonable utterance would have—and unless these men were blind to reason or brainless imbeciles, which they were not, they must have known the effect their words were producing, not only on the enemy but also on hundreds of our Dutch subjects in Cape Colony—I repeat that when a man knows this and still persists in his course of action, that man is just as guilty of sedition as the man who speaks sedition with the full intention of doing so, and is, to my mind, far more contemptible.

One thing I do know, and that is that the impression created on us soldiers in South Africa was one of profound astonishment and disgust that Englishmen could so far forget their duty towards their Sovereign and country as to make these seditious speeches. Treason appears to be a difficult matter to define, if one can judge from the many vicious statements which were allowed to pass without notice. I am perfectly well aware that I shall be told that it is our policy to treat these utterances with silent contempt; but to us in South Africa this policy seemed neither just nor sound when we saw the endless harm these effusions were causing, and will cause for a long time to come.

On top of all this came the lies spread broadcast

by certain continental papers.   One instance of this
which I saw will show to what lengths these un-
speakably coarse and cowardly attacks were carried.

" Seh nur wie der brave Englische soldat schlagt,"
as near as I can recollect, was the heading of a
picture that appeared in one of the leading German
illustrated papers, the name of which I cannot for
the moment remember.   It purported to represent
a Boer attack on a patrol of our men, who were
escorting a number of Boer women and children to
one of the concentration camps; to shield themselves, our Tommies *were holding the Boer women
and children in front of them.*   Can anyone conceive
a more abominable production?   It makes one's
blood boil to think of our brave and chivalrous
Tommy being subjected to these insults.   Of course,
we know why it was done.   What effect could it
possibly have on any young Dutchman, other than
to make him wish to seize a mauser and bandolier
and join the nearest commando?   This, at any rate,
was one potent influence in swelling the ranks of the
rebels.   How could it be otherwise?   What man,
not knowing the utter falsehood of these pictures,
could remain callous?   I have no hesitation in saying
that my sympathies are with the man who amid these
circumstances shouldered his rifle and risked his life.

This campaign of calumny against our troops at length got so bad that the Dutch and English throughout South Africa rose up and strongly protested against it.   I will give a typical instance —the meeting held in Bloemfontein in February 1902, presided over by Dr Kellner, who was one of the deputation that went out to surrender the town to Lord Roberts.   This resolution was proposed and carried unanimously: " We, the citizens of Bloemfontein, having had our attention drawn to certain statements made in England and on the Continent of Europe, accusing the British army of barbarous and wanton cruelty to defenceless women and children, take this opportunity of publicly denouncing such statements as wholly untrue, so far as our experience and knowledge of the conduct of the British troops in this part of the country is concerned.   We would further like to record our appreciation of the humanity and good conduct of all the troops passing through or stationed here, and our conviction that if there had been any truth in the slanders referred to, we should have been fully acquainted with the facts."

The resolution was proposed by a member of the late Government of the Orange Free State, and in doing so he said Bloemfontein must not keep silent, as it could speak more authoritatively than any other town in South Africa, and the whole world would look to it for refutation of the vile slanders.

Similar resolutions were passed all over the country, the residents of each town or district speaking for their own portion of the country. The result was that these slanders dropped.

There is not the slightest doubt that there was a thoroughly well-planned scheme to keep the Dutch in Cape Colony in a state of ferment. I could give many instances of the most blatant sedition preached throughout the Colony, the authors of which always managed to keep within the letter of the law. I shall not pursue this subject further, as I have no wish to rake up the past; but the pity of it is that the men who, by every despicable means in their power, swelled the Boer ranks, yet were too cowardly to take up arms themselves, could not have been punished in place of the men whom they drove into rebellion.

That many burghers were misled by the malicious statements, spread both in England and in the Colonies, we have been repeatedly told by the Boers themselves. " It is," said one of them, " your accursed cant of peace, of concession, of conciliation, of graceful surrender, of economy, and anti-militarism, which has brought war into Africa, and has destroyed my brethren and my property." The same man said the Boers had good foundation for the belief that could they hold out long enough our policy of 1881 would eventually prevail.

I have given some at least of the causes that helped to swell the Boer ranks and give them the hope of eventual success. Now I shall endeavour to show the means adopted by Steyn to keep his burghers in the field and raise their drooping courage.

The day after our occupation of Bloemfontein I went round with Captain Atcherley of the Army Service Corps, who was at that time supply officer to our brigade, to some of the stores in the town, in quest of supplies. In one store we came across a file of official war news which had been issued from day to day; after reading through some of it I tried to picture myself in the place of the few English who remained in Bloemfontein during the war and must have depended solely on these statements for news as to how the war was proceeding, and to imagine what their feelings must have been. I could come to no other conclusion than that they must have had a miserable time, and been filled with an agony of doubts and fears after reading nothing day after day but these reports of enormous British losses and Boer victories. Such a tissue of falsehoods it would be hard to imagine. This was the explanation, as far as I can remember, made to allay any uneasiness at our near approach to Bloemfontein—that it was a huge trap, carefully thought out and planned by the Boer leaders, to entice us into the country; then they would surround and capture the whole of our force. Of Cronje's capture I saw no mention whatever. Out of curiosity I began counting the numbers of British killed that were chronicled after each reported engagement. Very soon I counted no fewer than over 190,000—far more men than we at that time had in the whole of South Africa.

The report of the disembarkation of rooineks at Durban was rather funny. A harrowing picture was drawn of the British officers flogging their reluctant and weeping men ashore, who in a few days were to become food for the Boer mausers. One of the last fights chronicled was the battle at Driefontein, which was reported to have been a great Boer victory, and we were said to have left many thousands dead on the field. One incident in the fight, I remember, was the diffi- culty we were said to have had in making our soldiers attack the brave burghers. "The enemy, as a last resource," it continued, "turned their cannon on to their own infantry to make them advance, only to be shot down by our burghers in front." A truly pathetic picture for poor Tommy!

The Transvaal burghers evidently were kept supplied with news of a similarly entertaining description. On our occupation of Johannesburg we found the last issue of *The Standard and Digger's News*, describing the glorious Boer victory and utter rout of General French and his enormous army at Klipriversberg two days before. Thousands of the British dead and wounded, it informed its readers, were strewn all over the veldt.

The ending of the accounts of all these battles was invariably the same. This would be typical: "Utter defeat of the enemy and many cannon captured. The enemy left over seven thousand dead and wounded on the field. The burghers fought with great bravery, and lost only two killed and seven wounded. The enemy attacked in great numbers and with two hundred cannon."

I have not exaggerated the numbers in the least: if anything, I have erred the other way. With these stories dinned into their ears every day, and our prisoners of war passing through to Pretoria,

there was little cause for wonder that the Boer
hopes ran high. Our advance came as a thunderbolt to them. At first they did not and could not
realise it. The reports that filtered in were laughed
at. It was only the evidence of their own eyes
that brought home to them how they had been
befooled. There was no holding them then.
Steyn's authority collapsed like a house of cards. I
was told by a burgher that Cronje's surrender was
kept from them, and that they were living in such
a fool's paradise that any rumours of the disaster at
Paardeberg that reached them were not believed.
It was only our arrival at Bloemfontein that
brought the truth home to them.

I have an extract from a letter written by a
burgher which was published in January 1900 in
Cape Town by a Dutch paper, *Ons Land*. It is
quite mild in comparison with the official war news
published in Bloemfontein, and not worth noticing
except that it was by such statements as these,
published in the very capital of Cape Colony, and
spread among the Dutch colonists, that bitterness
was caused and incentives given to rebellion :—" In
the fight at Modder River, at Kimberley, we beat
them [the British] at every point ; their dead and
wounded lay for days on the battlefield. The

English themselves acknowledge that they lost more than 3000 men. We know now that it is more. At Colenso, Tugela, we completely crushed them. There they lost 5,070 killed and wounded [the odd 70 being added, I presume, to give the figures an appearance of great accuracy]. Truly, God fights our battles for us in this unrighteous war. Just imagine, they took seven of our doctors prisoners while they were tending our wounded on the battlefield, and removed them to Cape Town. On the way, among other things, they locked them up in a fowl-run, full of vermin, and made them travel in dirty cattle-trucks."

This is quite good, but feeble compared with many other statements which I have seen.

As a counterblast the following experience may be interesting :—

After the Sanna's Post disaster I travelled from Bloemfontein to Cape Town with a train full of Boer prisoners and our wounded. Poor Tommy, doubling up his wounded limbs as best he could, sat bolt upright on the narrow and hard seats of a third-class carriage while the Boer prisoners lolled back on the comfortable cushioned seats of the first-class carriages. I don't instance this with the remotest idea of expressing resentment at our sending down our prisoners of war in comfort, but merely to show with what consideration they were treated. I feel certain that had these burghers seen the discomfort some of our wounded were in, they would have been the first to give up their places to them.

I cannot do better than conclude this chapter and book by quoting an extract from the address presented at Bloemfontein by the loyal burghers of the Orange River Colony to Mr Chamberlain on his recent visit to South Africa. The address was signed by the following representative ex-burghers of the late Orange Free State :—

P. D. de Wet, ex-Generaal ;

F. Schimpers, Winburg ;

S. Jacobz, Senekal ;

C. J. Cloete, Bethlehem, late Member of the Volksraad ;

C. Bornman, Kroonstad, late Member of the Volksraad ;

S. Benkes, Vrede, late Member of the Volksraad ;

W. Richter, Vrede ;

Van Wyk, Vrede, late Member of the Volksraad ;

J. Els, J.P., Heilbron, late commandant ;

J. F. F. Cloete, Edenburg ;

F. H. Cloete, Edenburg ;

Dr Leech, Ventersburg ; and the Rev. Du Plessis, late of Lindley.

It begins as follows :—

" We, loyal Dutch residents and ex-burghers of the Orange River Colony who surrendered under Lord Roberts' proclamation when we realised that the Constitutional Government of the late Orange Free State had ceased to exist and that further warfare could not affect the result, but would certainly add further to the bloodshed and the ruin of the country, and who have kept our oaths, beg to thank you for according us an interview to enable us to place before you points in which those whom we represent are specially interested.

" We are aware that you are kindly receiving many deputations from the old residents of this country, but we feel that the special interests of our friends may perhaps not be fully represented by the delegates who have not been specially elected by our section of the people. We therefore respectfully claim the right to speak for ourselves and for those whom we represent, as we are satisfied with the Government, its actions, and its policy, and do not wish to ask for changes.

" We recognise that to-day all the residents of

18

the Orange River Colony are passively loyal to the Crown, but our past record does, we trust, entitle us to claim that we represent a section whose loyalty has been voluntarily assumed, and we cannot too strongly condemn any action which may keep alive or may again stir up the embers of dissension between Boer and Britisher.

"We note with the fullest appreciation your remark at Krugersdorp to the effect that the man who tries to separate us is our worst enemy."

After pointing out in the address some special points which, they thought, might benefit by Mr Chamberlain's consideration, they went on to say :—

"We are grateful for what has been done by the Government in its recognition of the loyal Dutch people whom we represent, and we beg that the Government will always recognise our desire to co-operate with its policy to further the prosperity of this colony, and to lay the foundations of a United South Africa under the British Flag."